LIVING WIT.. GOD
AND MONEY

BY

PHILIP EVANS

'Living with God and Money'
written by Philip Evans.

ISBN: 978-0-9543907-6-1.

Available from Amazon for Kindle: ASIN B01OOAJMY0.

Copyright © Philip Evans 2015.

The right of Philip Evans to be identified as author of this work has been asserted by him in accordance with the Copyright, Designs and Patents Act 1988.

First published by the author in 2015.
Philip Evans
13 Camborne Road, Welling, Kent, United Kingdom DA16 3LD

Contact Philip by e-mail at: philip.evans.gb@gmail.com

Printed by Western Printers
108 Cleveland Street, London, United Kingdom W1T 6NY

All rights reserved.

Scripture quotations are from The Holy Bible, English Standard Version® (ESV®), copyright © 2001 by Crossway, a publishing ministry of Good News Publishers. Used by permission. All rights reserved. Spellings have been anglicised and where parts of quotations are in italics the emphasis has been added by the author.

The cover design is by Su-Ann Foulds.
The cover illustrations are by Horace Knowles © The British and Foreign Bible Society 1954, 1967, 1972, 1995. Used by permission.

You are welcome to copy the text of this book for personal study or for circulation on a non-profit basis. For any other purpose, whether or not for profit, you will require written permission in advance from the author before copying, reproducing or transmitting extracts in any form or by any means, electronic or mechanical, including photocopying, recording or using any information storage and retrieval system.

Appreciation

I am grateful to many people for ideas and advice that have contributed to this book but especially to the staff and volunteers at All Souls Clubhouse Community Centre & Church, where I spent three very happy years developing financial capability training for Christians, and to my friend Emrys Lloyd-Roberts who read various drafts and offered many invaluable suggestions.

My former pastor at Westminster Chapel, Dr R T Kendall, very kindly wrote the Foreword. He is the person who has done most to teach me what it is to be a Christian and I am grateful that a theologian of his standing has affirmed that what I have written here is Biblically based.

I am grateful to God for the skills of an osteopath and the prayers of people around the world in restoring me to good health. I appreciate especially the prayers of my Parish Church, St Mary's, and of the pastors at the nearby Pentecostal Church, Freedom Centre International.

Information

This book was written primarily to be sold and circulated in electronic formats, which is why very many Scripture references are in included in the main text and not as footnotes or endnotes.

Handling money and dealing with money problems can be complicated in both personal and business life. Nobody involved in the writing or production of this book is responsible for any action you take, or fail to take, based on what is written in this book.

If you are worried about your financial situation, or struggling to live on your income or already in debt, you should consider getting independent expert advice as soon as possible. As debt is such a common problem around the world, you may be able to get **free** advice.

Living with God and Money

For a dreadful, a dreadful thing is the love of money, it disables both eyes and ears, and makes men worse to deal with than a wild beast, allowing a man to consider neither conscience, nor friendship, nor fellowship, nor the salvation of his own soul, but having withdrawn them at once from all these things, like some harsh mistress, it makes those captured by it its slaves. And the dreadful part of so bitter a slavery is, that it persuades them even to be grateful for it; and the more they become enslaved, the more doth their pleasure increase; and in this way especially the malady becomes incurable, in this way the monster becomes hard to conquer.

John Chrysostom
(345-407)

Living with God and Money

Contents

Foreword by R T Kendall

EVERY PERSON SHOULD read this book. Most forewords I write concern books that are aimed for a limited audience — whether for a church leader, a new Christian or a particular type of church member. But not this one. This book is for everybody, whether Christian or not, whether a church leader or layman.

It is about money. It is a no-joke book. It is serious stuff and urgently needed by all people. It will teach most people things about money they did not know they needed. It taught me a lot.

This book will give you a worldview about money, finances, the banking system and its relevance for the Church.

Many people sadly do not know how to handle money. That is a major reason so many people are in debt. I myself learned the hard way how to handle money — over 50 years ago — when I foolishly got deep into debt. It took years to get out of debt. I made a vow — which I have kept — never to owe money again to anybody.

You will possibly never have heard of Philip Evans. I first met him in May 1977, a few months after I began my ministry at Westminster Chapel, and from them onwards he followed my progress in the *Westminster Record* and would attend services occasionally. He became a member during the last quarter of my ministry there and when he would call at my vestry he would say interesting things about money. He warned of the global crisis that was at hand regarding banks throughout the world. He spoke how the nations need people to be in debt and how their economies would be destroyed if everybody instantly paid their debts! I wrote the Foreword to his first book, *Fleeing Babylon*, the day I retired as minister.

Philip writes as a layman, an evangelical Christian. All he says is Biblically based. It may surprise you to know that Jesus may have dealt with money more than any other subject. Philip brings out Biblical truths about money that I had not even thought of. I commend this book to you. It will open your eyes — as it has done mine — and will result in giving you a worldview about money generally and, should you need it, help you to learn how to handle money particularly.

Give this book to your friends. Spread the word. There is no need for everybody being swallowed up in the crisis at hand. Be prepared for it. This book could spare you of incalculable loss and grief.

Dr R T Kendall
Minister, Westminster Chapel, London
(1977—2002)

Preface

THIS BOOK EXAMINES what Jesus of Nazareth taught about money. He said a lot about the power of money and how to control it: in fact, he spoke about this more than almost anything else and, 2,000 years later, what he said still deserves our careful attention.

Although Jesus is remembered as a popular teacher arrested by the Jewish authorities as a heretic and executed by the Roman occupation as a dangerous dissident, few people today examine his teachings. His biographers record that at the time people were 'astonished' at what he said because he spoke with authority, unlike their usual teachers. The first officers sent to arrest him returned without him with the excuse, 'No one ever spoke like this man!'

Before he was a teacher, Jesus grew up in Nazareth working in the family carpentry business. Although not middle class by any modern definition, the family would have been relatively well off by comparison with many of their neighbours. Jesus later spoke about the role of money and wealth in society, using stories about landowners and merchants. I believe that more people today would be interested in Jesus if they knew more about what he taught.

Unlike the religious leaders who criticised Jesus' teaching, his authority did not come from wealth because he lived as a simple itinerant, supported by donations given by grateful followers. His ability to inspire did not come from family influence because they did not believe in him and his neighbours rejected him. His message did not come from scholarship because he had no academic training. It came from the integrity of his character and the authenticity of his lifestyle. Nobody can fake brilliance and authenticity. But the eternal significance of Jesus of Nazareth is that he defies a natural explanation.

It is widely thought that the 'Jesus of faith' is not the same as the 'Jesus of history': that is, the Jesus that people believe in today is not the real man who actually walked in ancient Israel. While that is often true, it should not be. Many people today believe fanciful things about Jesus of Nazareth, some the result of well-meaning exaggeration and some out of a desire to discredit him and his legacy. I believe that the Jesus we should believe in should be the same Jesus presented to us in the Bible, which I think accurately describes the Jesus of history.

Although I have written this book primarily for Christians, if you are a stranger to Christian teaching please keep in mind that the Bible is not really a book but a library. It is a collection of books written by about thirty different people over a period of about 1,500 years. It consists of history, theology, philosophy and poetry but, overall, it is a *religious* library, so that even the history of ancient Israel and the biographies of Jesus of Nazareth should be read as *religious* history. By that, I mean that they are the authors' experiences of God and therefore include different viewpoints and require various methods of interpretation.

I am not asking you to believe that what the Bible says about God is necessarily true or accurate. I believe it is but, if you do not believe as I do, I hope you will keep an open mind. All I am asking is that you take what the Bible says at face value and resist trying to judge it as history, philosophy or science. If that seems a very narrow view, please remember that various parts of the Bible have, for thousands of years, had a spiritual and moral impact on all sorts of people and we should not assume that our generation has outgrown our need of what it says.

So there is no misunderstanding, I should explain that this book is not about the technical skills necessary to handle money successfully: skills such as budgeting, banking and borrowing. Rather, I hope that it will help people develop a healthy relationship with money, to act more consistently with their own best interests and to relate with wisdom and deeper effectiveness to the people around them. And to be disciples of Jesus of Nazareth!

I also wish to emphasise three things that I usually explain before I teach about money. First, I do not want readers to feel guilty about the ways you have got and used money in the past. I think it goes without saying that if someone has behaved illegally or unethically, they should feel guilty: they should repent, offer restitution if that is possible and change their ways. But I do not want people to be too hard on themselves if they come to realise that they could have done things better. This is true of all of us!

Second, I find it useful to address the fear many people have that a 'Christian' view of money necessarily means a life of poverty. As I hope you will realise, while Christians should renounce extravagance and excess, and while we may be surprised at what Jesus teaches about coveting, he does not expect us to decline good food, shun nice clothes and never spend money on enjoying ourselves where we have the opportunity for these things.

Third, I think it unrealistic to say that there is a Christ-centred or specifically 'Christian' approach to money, to be adopted as an attitude or principal in some way separate to our routine approach to all of life. We cannot expect to identify a few principles of stewardship or generosity and 'bolt them' on to our existing lifestyle. That would be like thinking that we can have an approach to, say, driving a car that is distinct to who we are. There may be exceptions but, generally, an irresponsible or inconsiderate person will be a careless or thoughtless driver. It is usually the same with money and if we wish to handle it in ways that are pleasing to God then our entire lives will have to become pleasing to him.

I wrote this book during a long illness. I had decided to write it a few months before I realised that I was unwell in November 2013 and had already arranged to take a break from my usual activities from the start of 2014. The first draft, which I finished at Easter 2014, was what I had planned to write but it was very unsatisfactory. By Christmas, I had completely rewritten the book. I was checking what I thought was the final draft before circulating it to some friends when I realised that the chapter on coveting was quite inadequate. The book continued to evolve and now contains a lot of material that had not even occurred to me 20 months ago. I received my first effective medical treatment in January 2015 and expect this book to be published towards the end of a period of convalescence.

I intend *Living with God and Money* as a catalyst. If it finds an audience and opens up a better way of living, those who wish to should feel free to adapt the material for their own use.

Philip Evans
June, 2015

1: You cannot serve God and Money

No one can serve two masters, for either he will hate the one and love the other, or he will be devoted to the one and despise the other. You cannot serve God and money.
Matthew 6:24

JESUS SAID THAT we cannot serve both God and money. He said that not because we should not serve both but because it is impossible. Inevitably, we will end up loyal to one and despising the other. I have heard trying to serve both God and money to be like holding dual nationality in two countries that are at war with each other. Neither side will leave us alone; both want our allegiance!

Who is God? The word 'god' is used to describe all sorts of superhuman beings, some purely spiritual in nature and others, like the Greek and Roman deities, with physical bodies. It can also be used to refer to an exceptionally handsome or beautiful person, a superior athlete or a powerful ruler. 'God' spelled with an upper case 'G' usually refers to the God of the Bible.

In the Bible, the word for God is generally taken to refer to the creator God. It embraces the idea of God as Trinity — God the Father, God the Son and God the Holy Spirit — but generally refers to God the Father. When, for example, the Bible speaks of 'children of God', it does not mean children of the Son of God or children of God the Holy Spirit. It usually means God the Father, the Father of the Lord Jesus Christ and the one from whom the Holy Spirit comes in Jesus' Name and at Jesus' request.

In the Bible, God has a name. Jews think the name so holy that they never say it or write it in full. They sometimes omit the vowels and write the rest in capitals YHWH or the use a Latin version of the name, Jehovah. In many English Bibles, this name is written in capitals as LORD and I will follow that custom in this book.

The LORD is not only the creator who sustains the universe but he loves, saves, judges and rewards. He has told us how best to live our lives. In what Christians call the Old Testament, the Hebrew Scriptures revered by the Jews, he explains it in the first five books that are referred to collectively as the Torah. It is unfortunate that 'Torah' has come to be translated into English as 'Law' because it really means teaching, instruction and guidance. It is not like modern legislation or meant to be interpreted legalistically, which is why it is presented within the story of early human history and the founding of the Israelite nation. Although some of it was meant to be mandatory, it was intended as a source of wisdom and direction to be interpreted sensibly. It was, therefore, generally accepted that a farmer would feed and water animals and could pull one out of danger on the Sabbath, even though the Torah prescribed it as a mandatory rest day when the farmer should not do any work at all.

In the New Testament, most of the teaching is found in the biographies of Jesus, called Gospels, and the letters written by some of Jesus' earliest followers. Again, it was not meant to be new law or legislation for Jesus' followers but a description of principles, standards and lifestyle. The only mandatory commandments are the two that Jesus said summed up everything that God had expected of people in the past and everything he expected of his own followers. 'You shall love the Lord your God with all your heart and with all your soul and with all your mind and with all your strength. You shall love your neighbour as yourself.' However you interpret the first of those commandments, to love God with our entire being, *it is an exclusive commitment*. We cannot *also* serve money!

Some Bible translations quote Jesus as saying that we cannot serve both God and Money, with the capital M to emphasise that Money is like a person. Other translations have, 'God and mammon', which is the most accurate translation of all. Although 'God and money' conveys Jesus' meaning for 21st Century readers well enough, had he said exactly that someone in his original audience might have questioned his assumption that people serve money. The difference between money and mammon is therefore critical to understanding what Jesus meant.

Money was invented at various times in history in various parts of the world, as if for the first time, in order to help people to live together more easily. Money is a standard channel of exchange and a convenient means of storing wealth and it was only by using it that communities could expand and develop the public services that today we take for granted. But money evolved beyond a tool, even an indispensable tool. Mammon is money *personified*, money with influence that lures and drives us. The distinction between money and mammon would not have been lost to the people who listened to Jesus.

Jesus said that we cannot serve both God and money at least twice. The first time was in his Sermon on the Mount, his description of a lifestyle approved by God. I think he said it then because he did not want his hearers to be deterred from living the way he described by the financial consequences. The second time was when he confronted some Pharisees, members of the religious establishment of their day, who claimed to serve God but were lovers of money and, as a consequence, they were estranged from God, serving only money.

We can live in this world either serving God, living his way as described in the Bible, or we can serve money, the thing that most people today rely on to get things and to get things done. We cannot hope to do both!

* * *

We tend to think that money replaced barter, the exchange of goods and services, but this is not quite true. Money replaced credit and debt. Barter works successfully only when two people want to exchange goods of equivalent value at the same time but, more often than not, people had to stagger their exchanges. One person wanted wheat for bread while the other wanted milk for cheese but because they could not make the exchange simultaneously, one ended up debtor to the other.

Money therefore made life simpler for everyone. The first types of money did not need any intrinsic value of its own if everyone trusted and respected the system. People used everyday things like seashells and coloured beads successfully. A person who needed the wheat handed over some beads that the other person could exchange for milk later.

When the geographical areas within which people traded began to expand, money needed to have transferable wealth of its own. Silver rings were common. When we read in Genesis that Jacob's sons took bundles of money to Egypt, they were almost certainly silver rings of equal weight tied together in bundles of equal weight. Jewellery was made to be used as money: earrings and bracelets were a certain weight because it allowed them to be traded easily. In Babylon, the richest people stored their wealth as gold bars.

The first coins were made at Lydia in Asia Minor in around BC 678: the word 'money' derives from the name of the local goddess, Moneta. For centuries, coins were made of precious metals like bronze, silver and gold and so had value everywhere but gradually they began to be backed up by political rather than financial power. King Henry 8th of England was the first European ruler to replace the precious metal with cheaper alternatives. Today, the metal in a UK £1 coin is worth less than 4p. More recently, information technology has made it possible for money not to have *any* physical existence.

Most money today exists only as data in sophisticated banking systems. Coins, banknotes and other documents give a small percentage of money a reality in the real world but even that is only the same sort of reality as a novel: it is 'real' only in that it gives expression to the idea. What began as a system of trust, with local people respecting the way that beads or seashells represented the value of wheat and milk, is now more theoretical than ever. It works and is binding on almost everyone in the global village because without it life would be impossible.

Medical research has shown that making money can produce the same sort of 'high' as cocaine, by stimulating the same area of the brain. This goes some way to explaining the escalating selfishness, greed and recklessness that drives people to sacrifice their relationships, neglect their families and ruin their health for money they do not need. It also explains many gambling addictions and the reckless behaviour of bankers and financial traders who have plunged their employers into unrecoverable debt. Many 'wealth gurus' therefore advise people to define the lifestyle they want and then calculate how much money they need to be able to live it, rather than risk their mental and emotional well-being in chasing an abstract concept of wealth.

Our understanding of money's function and our attitudes towards it are formed very early in life, much earlier than most lifestyle values. Every child quickly learns to rely on money to get what he or she wants. As we grow older, money is what we think we need in order to be the person we want to be, to get on in society and to leave our mark on history. We therefore develop a quiet desperation to accumulate it.

We know that money cannot buy us love but while teaching in schools I met many young people who thought money was indispensable to falling in love, marrying, starting a family and achieving personal happiness. With so much at stake, it is no wonder that money problems are often more debilitating than problems with our health and relationships. Research has shown that people struggling with debt do not often relate well to their families and friends or function efficiently at work. Students worried about money have been found to do consistently worse than expected in their examinations.

I explained that 'real' money, like coins and bank notes, exist in the real world only like a novel. People try to make fiction real in many ways, such as biographies of fictional characters, like Sherlock Holmes, or tour guides to fictional places, like J R Tolkien's Middle Earth. Computer games and role-play can immerse us deeper into the experience. When people are obsessed with fiction, they can become unbalanced in real life: they cease to make clear distinctions about what is important or remember what is acceptable behaviour in the real world. In the same way, obsession with money often changes people, distorting their perceptions and priorities.

I would often begin personal finance lessons by asking the school pupils if there were particular careers they wanted to follow. Occasionally, some would say that they would do any job so long as it made them rich. I explained that although it is possible to get rich doing work we enjoy, pursuing wealth for its own sake changes people, and not for the better. That is the impact of mammon on human personality.

Mammon is money with influence. It gets into our thinking like leaven in bread, influencing our will, reason, imagination, conscience, impulses, habits, plans and choices. It subtly captivates every thought, feeling, love and aspiration, inflating them. When enough people began to give disproportionate importance to money, entire societies revolve around it. Everyone has little choice but to rely on money as it transforms and transfigures moralities, business, politics, opinions, customs and our very concept of civilization and democracy. This is mammon operating in the background of life.

Mammon finds expression through capitalism more readily than any other media. Capitalism is widely thought to be the same as free trade but there is a key difference. People have always traded for profit. Producing goods and offering services are natural ways to get what we need to live. Although there have always been greedy people, most people were satisfied to earn enough for their families to live in a degree of comfort. Among the things of greater importance than hoarding possessions was the amount of leisure time people could enjoy. If a farmer was to increase the hourly rate for his labourers gathering in a harvest, he was more likely to slow progress than hasten it because they would work only long enough to earn the same amount of money as before.

From time to time, however, a businessman would devote himself to commerce with an intensity alien to his contemporaries, desiring to maximise his own profit. His competitors had to respond in kind in order to stay in business. But when the catalyst, the greedy businessman, retired or died, business gradually returned to its previous pace.

Then Benjamin Franklin changed things forever. He was one of America's founding fathers and his picture is on its $100 banknote because he was its first home-grown, self-made millionaire. He thrived on hard work, enjoyed success and was able to retire young and promulgate his approach to business through a series of articles. The most famous of these are, *Necessary Hints to Those That Would be Rich* (1736) and *Advice to a Young Tradesman* (1748).

Franklin taught that money, not labour, created wealth and equated leisure with idleness. This rigorously rational approach to business began the legitimisation of avarice. Although people deplored Franklin's methodology as 'gaining wealth, forgetting all but self', gradually it became the only way to do business. Today we call it capitalism, and we tend to think that the only alternative is communism. But capitalism is not synonymous with trading for profit and Jesus taught a better way for everyone.

Reading this, it may seem like mammon has a personality, operating in the shadows like a pagan idol manipulating people. Many have thought this and it has moved generations of artists to portray mammon as a demon. But mammon's influence is really very much more ordinary. It is a cosmology, a means of explaining the nature and progress of life and, accordingly, the driving force of human society.

Mammon was a concept that originated in ancient Babylon, a place revered throughout history for its great wealth, culture, learning, self-indulgence and decadence. Today, Babylon is an archaeological site in modern Iraq, on the River Euphrates, about 60 miles south of Baghdad. It began as Babel, one of the earliest human settlements and the place where people tried to build a tower high enough to reach heaven in order to 'make a name' for themselves (Genesis 10:8-10 & 11:1-9). It later came to dominate two empires. Historians used to look back to ancient Rome or Greece for the seeds of modern civilisation but increasingly they now look even further back, to Babylon.

Some people think that Babylon was the first capitalist society and it seems to have operated as a debt economy, not too unlike our own. Most of the wealth in ancient Babylon was recorded on clay tablets, like most people's money today is recorded as computer data. It is likely that banking originated there.

There were no gods called mammon, no temples devoted to it, but the way of life in Babylon revolved around money as if it were the State religion. It is no different in today's world. Economic theory is a primary means of studying and explaining human life. Maximising profit is the legal goal of business and most moral choices are expected to be financially viable. Money itself is the global obsession, the status symbol that promises freedom, security, purpose, power, happiness — and even love! Some people make its accumulation their life's goal; others see it as the path to fulfilment or the things it can buy as defining their personality and social worth. Money is accepted as a force of nature, as irresistible as gravity, as unquestioned as evolution, pulling everything and everyone towards itself.

Jesus said that we cannot serve both God and money but he never said anything similar about other vices. He did not, for example, say, 'You cannot serve God and sex'. Nor did he say the more obvious, 'You cannot serve God and the devil'!

When Jesus discussed with scholars what was the greatest, or foremost, of God's commandments, the foundation on which people should build their lives, he identified two. 'You shall love the Lord your God with all your heart, with all your soul, and with all your mind... You shall love your neighbour as yourself. On these two commandments depend all the Law and the Prophets' (Matthew 22:35-40 & Mark 12:28-31). The phrase 'the Law and the Prophets' refers to the Torah, the ancient rule of life given by God to Moses about 1,500 years before, plus the writings of prophets who sought to bring the Israelites back to it when their allegiance to God had been compromised.

Jesus chose two commandments when asked to identify just one because although loving God is more important than loving people, as an ideal it can never stand alone. Loving God cannot be fulfilled apart from loving people. This is why Jesus said that the first and greatest commandment is to love God but the commandment to love our neighbour is like it or 'near to it': they may not be equal but they are inseparable.

Today we have no cause to doubt Jesus' wisdom. History is full of examples of people of all religions who claim to love God but who have been unbelievably cruel and vicious to people. Tragically, this is no less true of some people who claim to follow Jesus!

The most concise body of Jesus' teaching is the Sermon on the Mount. Although it does not contain these two commandments, it describes a lifestyle built upon their foundation. It describes how to love God and contains this summary of how we should treat people: 'Whatever you wish that others would do to you, do also to them, for this is the Law and the Prophets' (Matthew 7:12). This phrase is known as 'the Golden Rule'.

Concern for God and our neighbours should not be considerations that we place *just* ahead of every other consideration in life. They should be *far* ahead. Most people today, not only Christians, would say that they do put people first, ahead of money, and they would be sincere in saying so. But financial issues often come such a close second they divert attention and compromise our thinking and the ways we behave. I have experienced this in my own lifestyle choices and seen it in others. I have seen churches submit what they believe to be God's will to financial criteria, not quite believing that he will provide the resources but waiting for the money to be banked before taking any step of faith.

When Jesus confronted some Pharisees who claimed to serve God but loved money, recorded in Luke 14-16, he twice referred to 'unrighteous wealth'. The original Greek word translated wealth that Jesus used is really the word for mammon. We will look closely at this confrontation in a later chapter but now I want only to focus on the phrase, 'unrighteous wealth' because it is important to remember that wealth is not fundamentally, inherently unrighteous. But mammon is always unrighteous!

Some Pharisees accumulated their wealth illegally or unethically. On another occasion, Jesus accused them of neglecting both justice and mercy and of devouring widows' houses. That sort of behaviour was bad enough but what made their wealth *profoundly* unrighteous was the way they loved it and used it for their own glorification. Even when they gave to the poor, they turned the occasions into public pageants. In the Sermon on the Mount, Jesus warned his followers not to copy them, 'When you give to the needy, sound no trumpet before you, as the hypocrites do in the synagogues and in the streets, that they may be praised by others...' (Matthew 6:2-4).

When Jesus confronted the Pharisees face to face, he told them to use their unrighteous wealth to make friends for eternity. He was not implying that they should continue to accumulate more and more, only that they should use what they already had by making restitution and relieving poverty. I think it right to assume that Jesus meant them to do it modestly, discreetly, so that their Father who sees in secret would reward them.

An early follower of Jesus who contributed most to the New Testament was Paul of Tarsus. In a letter to his protégé, Timothy, he warned of the consequence of loving money and wanting to be rich. This is the passage from 1 Timothy 6:9-11.

Those who desire to be rich fall into temptation, into a snare, into many senseless and harmful desires that plunge people into ruin and destruction. For the love of money is a root of all kinds of evils. It is through this craving that some have wandered away from the faith and pierced themselves with many pangs.

The desire to be rich drives people to work long hours at jobs they do not like for money they do not really need. It propels them into dishonesty and illegality, cheating people about the quality of goods and services they offer and evading responsibility for problems. At extremes, it plunges many into destructive trade such as prostitution, pornography, people trafficking, drugs and child abuse.

The same desires, as well as the ambition to appear to be wealthier than is the case, traps many in irresponsible spending. We have only to look around to see how people not only spend the money they have but borrow more in order to indulge their pleasures and boast their extravagance. Every now and then, the news media highlight specific instances of gross hedonism, such as when city financiers celebrating their massive pay bonuses spend many tens of thousands of pounds on expensive wine and food in a single night.

Rich people have always behaved like this. F Scott Fitzgerald's important novel, *The Great Gatsby*, illustrates this very well. I think it continues to be a popular bestseller today because it resonates with many people's lifestyle aspirations. It is about a poor boy who gets rich in dubious ways in order to win a former sweetheart who married for money. Gatsby buys a great mansion with rooms he never enters, a library of books he never reads, expensive clothes he never wears and a swimming pool he does not use until the day of his death. He throws extravagant parties he does not like for people he does not know.

Poor people who aspire to be rich can behave just as badly. In the book, Myrtle lives above a run-down garage with her lifeless husband in a desolate place called the Valley of Ashes. But she is the mistress of the enormously wealthy Tom Buchanan. When Myrtle gets to New York with her lover, she spends his money as frivolously as if it were her own and, making herself the centre of attraction at a party, affects pompous elegance. She even demeans the 'lower orders', like the elevator boy she sends to buy ice for their drinks.

You may not be as obvious or arrogant as Myrtle but there is danger if you envy wealth. Psalm 73 begins with this warning, 'Truly God is good to Israel... But as for me, my feet had almost stumbled, my steps had nearly slipped. For I was envious of the arrogant when I saw the prosperity of the wicked...' When the author realised his predicament, and got close to God again (literally, he 'went into the sanctuary of God'), he could see the true situation: 'Truly you set them in slippery places; you make them fall to ruin...'

The characters in *The Great Gatsby* epitomise 'conspicuous consumption'. The term was first used in the late 19th Century in justifying the right of rich people to use their money for no better purpose than to enhance their status as 'gentlemen of leisure'. But history has seen even worse examples of rich people showing off in even more reckless and ridiculous ways. In some societies, it has been customary for the rulers to destroy great wealth — food, clothes and valuable items — just to show that they were so rich they did not need them. When this vanity destruction became a contest between neighbouring rulers, some would plunge their people into poverty rather than allow a rival to 'win'!

We may think such evil recklessness far worse than what we see today. But I am not so sure! Was it worse than paying bankers and financiers fantastic salaries and bonuses to lavish on luxuries and entertainments while people committed to healthcare and education often struggle to live modestly on their salaries?

It is no wonder that Paul described the love of money as the root of all evil! At least, that is what past generations of Christians thought Paul meant: that there is *one* root of *all* evil and it is avarice, the love of money. That is what I refer to as the traditional meaning of Paul's words found in 1 Timothy 6:10. The first translations of the Bible into English by Wycliffe (1348), Tyndale (1526) and Coverdale (1535) all interpret Paul's words, as covetousness is the root of all evil. The Geneva Bible (1560), the Bishops' Bible (1568) and the Douai-Rheims Version (1609), the main translations of the Protestant Reformation and the Roman Catholic Counter-Reformation, then made a distinction between the love of possessions (covetousness) and the love of money (avarice) to say that the desire or love of money is the root of all evil. After the Authorised (King James) Version (1611) put, 'The love of money is the root of all evil', the phrase became one of the most famous quotations in the English language.

Modern translations tend to describe the love of money as *a* root of *all kinds* of evil, allowing for other roots and other evils not associated with money. This is how the American Standard Version (1901), Revised Standard Version (1952), New King James Bible (1982), New International Version (1984), Good News Bible (1992), English Standard Version (2001) and others dilute Paul's unqualified statement. I accept that they have valid translations because the Greek words that Paul used can be translated either way. But after fifteen years studying both the love of money and the root of evil, I believe the traditional translation is what Paul meant. The love of money is the root (the *only* root) of *all* evil. We can see this when we look at the Bible's explanation of the origin of evil.

Babylon's most famous ruler was Nebuchadnezzar, who the Israelite prophet Isaiah likened to Lucifer. The name, Lucifer, means a bright morning star and he was God's favourite angel until he rebelled against God. He is now better known as Satan or the devil. This is the prophet's description found in Isaiah 14:12-15.

How you are fallen from heaven, O Day Star, son of Dawn! How you are cut down to the ground, you who laid the nations low! you said in your heart, 'I will ascend to heaven; above the stars of God I will set my throne on high; I will sit on the mount of assembly in the far reaches of the north; I will ascend above the heights of the clouds; I will make myself like the Most High. But you are brought down to Sheol, to the far reaches of the pit.

Lucifer had it all. Or almost! His ambition was to be like God. He did not want to *be* God but to be *like* God. He wanted autonomy and self-sufficiency; he did not want all that he had and enjoyed in dependence on God but he wanted it with independence. He did not, obviously, use money as we know it but a tool is defined by what it does, not by what it is called. Money is a tool used for valuing goods and services and of exchanging them in order to get things and get things done. Today we use pieces of metal, small sheets of paper and computer data. I cannot say what Lucifer used but, whatever it was, it was effective, so that he had begun to realise his ambition and many angels followed him when he was banished from heaven.

When the Bible explains the origin of evil in the world, it has the devil, in the guise of a serpent, tempting Eve with the same ambition: to be *like* God. Genesis 3 tells how the devil tricked Eve into doubting God's good intentions and thinking that by forbidding them to eat the fruit of the tree of the knowledge of good and evil that God was preventing them from being like him. 'For God knows that when you eat of it your eyes will be opened, and you will be *like God*, knowing good and evil.' The effectiveness of this tactic should not surprise us because the Bible tells us that God created Adam and Eve in his own image, to be *like him* (Genesis 1:27). But God did not create them to be autonomous, to pursue their own ambition in selfishness. This was sin at its most fundamental!

History remembers King Nebuchadnezzar as the ruler who did most to expand and beautify Babylon, to secure its reputation as the centre of learning and luxury. It was also his desire to conquer the holy city of Jerusalem. He was increasingly proud and vain and greedy for still more glory until God taught him humility, as Isaiah had prophesised. Nebuchadnezzar tells what happened in his own words, preserved in Daniel 4.

When the devil tempted Jesus in the wilderness, as described in Matthew 4:1-11 and Luke 4:1-13, it was to provoke this same sort of self-sufficiency and self-fulfilment. But the devil failed! Peter later wrote of Jesus: 'He committed *no* sin...' (1 Peter 2:22).

Paul's use of the metaphor, the *root* of all evil, is graphic. Most roots are ugly tangles that grow underground, out of sight, from where they feed flowers and fruit that are very different. The love of money is a root that grows in our unconscious minds, out of sight and rarely thought about, that feeds our desires. We see some of its fruit and flowers in the greed, vanity, excess, pretention, ostentation, snobbery, selfishness and so many other vices that the contemporary celebrity culture admires as virtues.

This root had poisoned the religious establishment in Jerusalem and would soon infect the Christian church. At Jerusalem, husband and wife, Ananias and Sapphira, sold some land but lied about donating the entire amount they got for it (Acts 5). Paul criticised Christians at Corinth who were cheating each other in business and exposing it through the courts (1 Corinthians 6:1-11). Demas left Paul's ministry team because he was 'in love with this present world' (2 Timothy 4:10). James' epistle is not addressed to just one church but to many and the problems he addressed were commonplace, including preferential treatment to rich people attending meetings, despising the poor and cheating employees to the point of withholding their wages. James also warned that the boasting of the Christian businesspeople who made their plans for prosperity without reference to God was not just arrogant but 'evil' (James 4:13-17). This should serve as a warning to Christian businesspeople today who make their business decision on no other basis than profit and loss. I am not suggesting that their decisions are illegal, immoral or unethical: only that they are essentially financial.

Jude's letter and Jesus' letter to Pergamum in Revelation 2 both condemn Christians for following Balaam's example of trying to use spiritual gifts for financial gain (compare Numbers 22-24 & 31:16, Jude 11 & Revelation 2:12-17). In his letter to Titus, Paul warned him about Christian teachers 'who are insubordinate, empty talkers and deceivers...upsetting whole families by teaching for shameful gain what they ought not to teach' (Titus 1:10-11). This is no doubt why Paul sets out the qualities for people eligible for church leadership in two of his letters. Among other criteria, 1 Timothy 3:1-13 and Titus 1:5-9 direct that overseers (or bishops) should not be lovers of money and deacons should be not greedy for dishonest gain. Older translations of the Bible use the phrase, 'not given to filthy lucre', an old-fashioned term that I think expresses exactly what Paul meant. Lucre is disreputable profit and the word could be used alone to convey Paul's meaning but 'filthy lucre' reinforces the sleazy, repugnant nature of the profit.

As money has become more important to society generally, it has eroded our shared concepts of honesty. In *The Great Gatsby*, the link between avarice and mendacity is clear. Gatsby is a criminal who mixes with criminals, like Meyer Wolfsheim. Jordon Baker cheated to win her first golf tournament. Daisy (the woman Gatsby idolises) and her enormously wealthy husband live as self-obsessed hypocrites, careless of their impact on others: 'they smashed up things and creatures and then retreated back into their money or their vast carelessness...and let other people clean up the mess they had made'. Even the book's narrator, Nick Carraway, is tainted by the family wealth he enjoys, which is the result of his great uncle evading his call to fight in America's Civil War to start a business. The businesspeople and artists who flocked to Gatsby's parties are freeloaders: few of them knew or cared to know their generous host and only one attended his funeral.

While society has always tolerated small acts of opportunistic dishonesty, the bounds of acceptable dishonesty are continually being pushed back. Putting false information on credit applications and inventing insurance claims is widespread today. Most people admit to pilfering from employers, restaurants and hotels. In many of the schools where I taught, many pupils saw nothing wrong in downloading music and movies illegally and thought those who paid for legal downloads were fools. Our default position when buying goods and services is to expect to be overcharged for poor quality or subject to terms and conditions that were not obvious. Whenever we complain about faulty goods or deficient work, we can expect to be treated with suspicion, as if making it up to get undeserved compensation. Some time ago, I saw a survey on honesty that considered shoplifting more no more dishonest than exceeding the speed limit on roads. For many people today, behaviour is not restrained by what is illegal or immoral but only by the chance of being caught!

We see such moral expediency mirrored in the last book of the Bible, called Revelation. It is called that because it opens with the words, 'The revelation of Jesus Christ, which God gave him to show to his servants the things that must soon take place'. Another name for the book is Apocalypse, an older word that today is associated with catastrophe but really means an unveiling or the discovery of something mysterious. What is the mystery? It is how creation operates and how things will pan out ultimately.

A recurring image in Revelation is a global trading system called Babylon, based on ancient Babylon. Five features of this global Babylon described in chapters 17-18 should make us think seriously about the global economic system today.

> **Babylon rides the nations.** The nations are symbolised in the vision by the beast with many heads that Babylon rides. Governments, not financial institutions, are supposed to run countries but while governments struggled to control financial organisations following the economic catastrophe of 2007/08, they found their own credit worthiness downgraded. In the vision, Babylon is 'the great city that has dominion over the kings of the earth'!

> **Babylon is a prostitute!** It appears as a glamorous woman, 'arrayed in purple and scarlet, and adorned with gold and precious stones and pearls' but commits fornication with the world's rulers. Babylon is, in fact, 'the mother of prostitutes': its fornication is not sexual but spiritual; the love of money that it arouses is the root of all evil.

> **Babylon is drunk.** It is 'drunk with the blood of the saints and with the blood of the martyrs of Jesus'! Being drunk with blood is an ancient metaphor for relentless, violent warfare that is never satisfied. A warlord

who not only defeated an enemy army but also needlessly slaughtered innocent civilians would be said to be drunk with blood. For Babylon to be drunk with the blood of Jesus' followers is a graphic way of describing its violent rejection of God's ways and God's people.

Babylon is a haven for evil! For over 100 years, the phrase 'business is business' has expressed the assumption that society's usual standards of morality do not apply to business. While there are businesspeople who knowingly act illegally and unethically, there are many more who suppose (in so much as they think about it at all!) that they are operating within industry norms. Worse, dishonesty is often a status symbol, identifying someone is a 'player' to be taken seriously: 'If you ain't cheating', some say, 'you ain't trying'.

Babylon's fall is total. It is as complete as the fall of ancient Babylon in the 7th Century. When that city finally crumbled to dust, for 1,000 years nobody could even tell where it had stood. The Hebrew prophet Jeremiah described ancient Babylon using imagery very similar to what we read in Revelation and to symbolise the completeness of its fall the scroll on which he first wrote it was sunk in the River Euphrates (see Jeremiah 51). The fall of Revelation's Babylon is demonstrated by an angel hurling a great stone into the sea.

A final thing to reflect on is God calling his people to leave this Babylon before it falls.

> *Come out of her, my people,*
> *lest you take part in her sins,*
> *lest you share in her plagues;*
> *for her sins are heaped high as heaven,*
> *and God has remembered her iniquities.*

It was reading this passage in 1996 that challenged me to start thinking more seriously than ever about the financial implications of Jesus' teaching. The issue for me was not God's call to his people to leave Babylon but why they needed it. Surely, looking around at the corruption and evil, they should have left of their own accord! I expect they stayed because they grew up there and could see nothing wrong, having also become a little drunk.

Like the image of Babylon as a glamorous woman, the lifestyle of the rich and those who wanted to be rich that Scott Fitzgerald portrayed looked good from a distance but it was decadent and hypocritical. The parties that made 'a Christmas tree of Gatsby's enormous garden' looked exhilarating but were not good places to be when sober. Nick Carraway found himself isolated and alone at the first one he attended and began to enjoy himself only when he started to drink. 'I had taken two finger-bowls of champagne and the scene had changed before my eyes into something significant, elemental and profound.'

God's call to his people in Babylon made me begin to think about what I may be overlooking and whether I had, as Americans say, 'drunk the kool-aid'. Christians living in capitalist, consumer societies may not live as selfishly ruthless as many other people, and we may be more modest and generous in how we use money, but we can still be unaware of the extent to which we have become a little intoxicated by Babylon's ways and blinded to our predicament. If we remain in Babylon, we will lose everything, along with everyone else, when the system falls. How do we 'come out of' Babylon? We turn from its ways and follow God's ways.

It is clear from the early chapters of Acts that, notwithstanding the problems that developed later, the first Christians experienced a revolution in the ways they related to and used money and wealth. Luke explains in Acts 2:42-47 what then happened.

> *They devoted themselves to the apostles' teaching and the fellowship, to the breaking of bread and the prayers... And all who believed were together and had all things in common. And they were selling their possessions and belongings and distributing the proceeds to all, as any had need. And day by day, attending the temple together and breaking bread in their homes, they received their food with glad and generous hearts, praising God and having favour with all the people. And the Lord added to their number day by day those who were being saved.*

These first disciples did not give up the concept of private property but they opened their homes to one another and shared everything. Their way of life was something less than a commune but more communal than the quality of generosity most churches experience today. They seemed to embrace the ancient Jewish principle that God owned everything and they were temporary stewards of the goodness he had given them to enjoy.

We should consider carefully the examples of Christians who sold their possessions and goods and gave the proceeds to help the poor. I doubt they sold *everything* but only what they did not want or need. I do not think they routinely sold land that was worked by people, so depriving those people of employment and the means to live. Instead, think that they managed it for the benefit of all, like Boaz, the 'hero' of the story of Ruth. I recommend reading the story Old Testament book of Ruth, not as a love story or an illustration of redemption but to see how Boaz treated people.

One exception seems to have been Joseph, who became known as Barnabas because he encouraged new believers: Barnabas means 'son of encouragement'. He was a Levite who had been born and brought up in Cyprus, where he owned land.

This implies that he was rich. At the end of Acts 5, we read that he sold this land and gave the proceeds to the apostles to distribute to people in need. I think Barnabas did this *because* he was a Levite.

The Levites were the tribe who looked after the Tabernacle and the Temple and, so that they could concentrate on this duty, they were the only tribe in Israel not permitted to own land but were given places to live and a share of the people's offerings. It therefore seems to me that Barnabas sold the land that his family should never have bought.

A former magician called Simon was an early Christian who misunderstood the importance of money. His story is told in Acts 8. When two apostles, Peter and John, laid their hands on some new Christians for them to receive the Holy Spirit, something remarkable happened that fascinated Simon. We do not know exactly what happened, although we can make some assumptions from Acts' record of similar events, but whatever happened, Simon misunderstanding the situation, offered the apostles money, asking, 'Give me this power also, so that anyone on whom I lay my hands may receive the Holy Spirit'.

Simon's offer is usually interpreted as a clumsy attempt to buy a spiritual gift and, ever since, his name describes the practise of buying positions of responsibility in the church: 'Simony'. But I think that Simon himself has been misunderstood. Sorcery is included in Paul's 'works of the flesh' listed in Galatians 5:19-21, and so it is not necessarily occultic but involve only conjuring and potions. As a magician, Simon would have been particularly perceptive and psychologically alert: what today we might call a mentalist. I think that he observed a link between a right attitude to material wealth and spiritual authority but misread the nature of the link. I think he was asking just how generous he needed to be in order to be worthy of the same spiritual authority. He was, of course, wrong to think like that but many Christians today seem to make a similar mistake and hope that by being generous they can win God's favour. We will explore why this is a mistake in a later chapter.

The characters in *The Great Gatsby* live fictitious lives but many people alive in the world today live lives that are no more real. Scott Fitzgerald called his book, *The Great Gatsby*, because the narrator, Nick Carraway, thinks that Gatsby is the most hopeful person he ever met. He thinks this largely because Gatsby never gave up his pursuit of a dream — a romantic dream — that constantly receded before him. Applying this persistence to life, Carraway closes the book with the belief that although dreams elude us, 'that's no matter — tomorrow we will run faster, and stretch out our arms farther...'

This is the illusion that mammon and money keeps many people pursuing in real life today, so they never perceive something better. But God offers something better, something tangible, something attainable in this life and in the next.

2: Only with difficulty will a rich person enter the Kingdom of God

Truly, I say to you, only with difficulty will a rich person enter the kingdom of heaven. Again I tell you, it is easier for a camel to go through the eye of a needle than for a rich person to enter the kingdom of God."
Matthew 19:23-24

WEALTH KEEPS OUR perceptions and aspirations anchored in the material world; it keeps us occupied with secondary things. When we know where our next meal is coming from, we worry about how it will taste; when we have many clothes to choose from, we fret about our image; when we are confident of making the next mortgage or rent payment, we consider redecorating or upgrading; when our furniture is comfortable, we think about how it looks; when we accumulate too many possessions, we buy storage; when we have too much leisure time, we strive for novelty. We focus on the finite and miss entirely the infinite.

When we do begin to think of 'spiritual' aspects of life, we usually think of our appreciation of literature, music and art. These are the human capacities that money cannot buy, although it can fake them. Rich people who do not appreciate art will nevertheless pay a lot of money for art that will impress the people who do appreciate it. Large business corporations will donate huge sums of money to art in order to improve their branding. But the spiritual realm is still a step beyond.

Although the ability to appreciate art does distinguish us from animals, and while it is evidence that we are created in God's own image, it is only by being 'born again' that we are able to see and enter the spiritual dimension. Hebrews 11, the Bible's great passage about faith, explains that, 'Without faith it is impossible to please him, for whoever would draw near to God must believe that he exists and that he rewards those who seek him' (Hebrews 11:6). For that to happen, among other considerations, we need to transfer the trust we have in money to God alone.

Jesus described how hard it is for a rich person to enter the Kingdom of God after meeting a rich young ruler. The young man had approached Jesus with a profound question: 'What must I do to inherit eternal life?' This story is important enough to be included in three of the four Gospels and a great deal depends on our doing better than the young man did.

Even after people are born again and commit themselves to living as Jesus' disciples, their old ways of thinking and behaving can be difficult to shake. In some of his parables, Jesus likened the deceitfulness of riches, the cares of this world, the pleasures of life and the desire for things to thorns that choke the Word of God and spiritual growth.

We may not consider ourselves to be rich compared to the people we see on television and in magazines, but many of us are rich when compared to our parents and grandparents and to a great many people living today in the poor regions of the world. But even if you are poor, either by the standards of most of the people you live among, or in an absolute sense that you cannot afford to pay for a healthy lifestyle, if you aspire to be rich then you may be making things just as difficult for yourself as someone who is rich. This is because *the love of money* is the root of all evil. 'It is through this craving', Paul wrote in 1 Timothy 6, 'that some have wandered away from the faith and pierced themselves with many pangs'.

If it really is easier for a camel to do something so impossible as to go through the eye of a needle than for a rich person to enter the Kingdom of God, we should not be complacent that we are really 'in'! Even if we are sure that we are in the Kingdom, we might not have made as much progress as we like to think if money chokes our spiritual growth and development. This spiritual hazard is why Jesus taught so much about money and wealth!

* * *

The story of the rich young ruler is recorded in Matthew 19:16-30, Mark 10:17-31 and Luke 18:18-30. I doubt it was the first time he had asked his question about eternal life to a spiritual teacher, or that he had ever received an answer that satisfied him. He may have taken the courage to ask again when he saw Jesus' openness and kindness in welcoming young children. At first, Jesus gave the young ruler what was probably the same reply he had heard many times before: keep the commandments. By that, Jesus meant living the sort of life defined by the Ten Commandments listed in Exodus 20 and Deuteronomy 5, including honouring parents and not murdering, committing adultery, theft, fraud or perjury. It is possible that Jesus added something new to what other teachers had replied, as Matthew's concludes the list with loving your neighbour as yourself.

The young man replied that he had done all this since his childhood and Jesus did not seem to doubt it. As a Jew, the man was not claiming any moral or religious perfection, free from all sin and wrongdoing, only that he had lived a sincere and devout life. Jesus then said something radical, 'But you lack one thing', and told him to give away all his wealth to the poor, so that he would have treasure in heaven, and to follow with his disciples.

Treasure in heaven is the subject of a later chapter but we should pause to understand what is meant in this story by 'eternal life', 'kingdom of heaven', 'kingdom of God', 'the new world' and 'the age to come'. While I do not think those terms are necessarily synonymous, they all refer to a future realm when the laws of Heaven will be established in the world. Although the Bible contains many indications of what this will be like, it does not define the Kingdom in concrete terms and people interpret it in different ways.

Both John the Baptist and Jesus began their ministries by telling people that the Kingdom was near at hand and the book of Acts closes with Paul in Rome preaching and teaching about the Kingdom.

We read in the Gospels of faithful Jews like Joseph of Arimathea who were waiting for the Kingdom of God. This devout ruler was among them. He was not complacent about his worthiness and readiness for it but we should be surprised that Jesus told him, 'One thing you lack'. Just **one**!

Some have assumed from Jesus' words that the man lacked poverty and conclude that being poor is the preferred situation for all 'true' Christians. This, however, cannot be correct because there is nothing in the Bible to suggest that it is wrong to be wealthy and both the Old and New Testaments mention wealthy people who were faithful to God. A woman called Tabitha was raised from the dead because she was respected as someone 'full of good works and acts of charity' (Acts 9:36). Cornelius, a Roman centurion, was noticed by God not only for his prayers but also for his gifts to the poor (Acts 10:4 & 31). The sin is not in having wealth but in loving and serving it.

The thing the devout ruler lacked was trust: unequivocal trust in God. Jesus' words revealed that the man's trust in God was incomplete and that he could not bring himself to complete it by transferring to God alone the trust he had in his inherited wealth. The only way for him to demonstrate that transfer of trust was by giving away his wealth.

As the rich young ruler walked away, sorrowful, Jesus told his disciples just how hard it is for a rich person to enter the Kingdom of God: harder than for a camel to crawl through the eye of a needle! This startled the disciples: 'Who then can be saved?' they asked. I expect they were thinking of themselves because none of them had come from poor families. Like Jesus himself, they were from relatively stable families with businesses or inherited wealth.

At least six of the disciples were fishermen. James and John were the sons of Zebedee, who owned a fishing fleet. Peter and Andrew were brothers in the family that may have been Zebedee's business partners. The families may well have lived in large houses on the shore of the Sea of Galilee. Matthew was a tax collector, a government official with a lucrative career. Simon is called a zealot, which suggests he was a politician; Judas Iscariot may also have been politically active: if this is correct, it is a strong indication they came from wealthy families.

Jesus assured his disciples that what is impossible for people is possible for God. Sometime later, they saw the truth of this when Jesus met Zacchaeus, a rich tax collector who had prospered from the corrupt practices of his profession. His remarkable story is told in Luke 19:1-10.

As Jesus entered Jericho, a crowd gathered. Zacchaeus was a short man who could not see what was going on and, because of his reputation, nobody would let him through to the front of the crowd. He therefore ran ahead of the crowd and climbed a tree. As Jesus passed by the tree, he paused, looked up, and asked to stay at Zacchaeus' house.

We do not know what Jesus and Zacchaeus talked about but we know the result: Zacchaeus publicly promised to give half of his possessions to the poor and to repay four times as much to everyone he had cheated. Did this amount to what Jesus had told the rich young ruler to do: to give away everything? I think it did but, in any event, Zacchaeus was an accountant who knew that his decision meant the end of his affluent lifestyle, especially if he began to do his job honestly. He realised that money would not be nearly as important to him anymore.

Jesus' responded to Zacchaeus' commitment by telling the crowd, 'Today salvation has come to this house...' Did Zacchaeus hear what the rich young ruler had wanted to hear? If he did, it was because Zacchaeus was prepared to do what the ruler would not.

Turning to Jesus in repentance is not necessarily an instant cure for everything wrong in our lives. Sometimes it is. Some new Christians are immediately freed from drug addiction, alcoholism, pornography, a short temper or a spending addiction. More often than not, however, deliverance involves a hard struggle because the seed of spiritual life within us grows gradually.

Jesus often told parables about a man sowing seed and the Gospels record three similar ones: Matthew 13:1-9 & 18-23, Mark 4:1-9 & 13-20 and Luke 8:5-8 &11-15. This is Matthew's account.

A sower went out to sow. And as he sowed, some seeds fell along the path, and the birds came and devoured them. Other seeds fell on rocky ground, where they did not have much soil, and immediately they sprang up, since they had no depth of soil, but when the sun rose they were scorched. And since they had no root, they withered away. Other seeds fell among thorns, and the thorns grew up and choked them. Other seeds fell on good soil and produced grain, some a hundredfold, some sixty, some thirty. He who has ears, let him hear...

Hear then the parable of the sower: When anyone hears the word of the kingdom and does not understand it, the evil one comes and snatches away what has been sown in his heart. This is what was sown along the path. As for what was sown on rocky ground, this is the one who hears the word and immediately receives it with joy, yet he has no root in himself, but endures for a while, and when tribulation or persecution arises on account of the word, immediately he falls away. As for what was sown among thorns, this is the one who hears the word, but the cares of the world and the deceitfulness of riches choke the word, and it proves unfruitful. As for what was sown on good soil, this is the one who hears the word and understands it. He indeed bears fruit and yields, in one case a hundredfold, in another sixty, and in another thirty.

A man goes to sow seed on an area of uncultivated, common land. He is not a farmer, just a man with some other occupation exercising his right to grow a small crop on common land to feed his family. The ground was not well prepared like on a farm and so some seed fell by the public footpath, some fell on rocky ground and some among thorns. Some, however, fell on to good soil and grew to maturity to produce a crop of up to hundredfold — that is, 1,000%! When Jesus later explained the parable, he likened the thorns that choked growth to the deceitfulness of riches, the cares of this world, the pleasures of life and covetousness that choke the Word of God and spiritual growth.

In between telling the parable to the gathered crowd and explaining its meaning to his immediate disciples, Jesus explained why he taught with parables (Matthew 13:12-15). It was because the people who listened to him did not understand the mysteries of the Kingdom of God, because their hearts were dull, their ears deaf and their eyes closed. But although they had shut themselves off from the Kingdom, Jesus wanted them to understand something — something that would give them a foothold. As Jesus explained, 'Whoever has, to him more will be given, and he will have abundance'. If his audience could grasp just one aspect of the truth, it would be their entrance into much more, with each new truth a stepping-stone into greater truth.

A person who becomes a Christian may know very little about the God of the Bible, Jesus the Son, the Holy Spirit or about the nature of salvation. But what they do know is their starting point. Grasping one truth, the Holy Spirit can help them to grasp more. Among the cultural issues, which often take a very long time to see, is the impact of money on spiritual development.

One reason for this is the guidance given when people first commit to Jesus Christ. Too often, it is all about ideology and very little about lifestyle. It sets out some key beliefs and encourages them to find a 'good' church and begin attending the services, to read the Bible and to pray each day. It may encourage them to find a group of Christians to meet with once or twice a week for friendship and mutual support. It may also seek to inspire them to help with evangelistic or charitable activities, like youth clubs, single parent groups and pensioners' lunches. While there is nothing at all wrong with this advice, it stops short and does not help them examine their lifestyle values. It can even leave the impression that to be a Christian requires no more than to insert some beliefs, personal devotions and charitable work into a lifestyle that carries on pretty much as before.

We might expect that when new Christians begin reading the Bible and attending church, they would soon realise how different the lifestyle that Jesus and his apostles taught is from what they are use to. But I hear too many sermons encouraging us to rely on God and live faithfully but without much specific guidance about what this requires, beyond the idea of doing good. As so many generations of Christians have grown up with capitalism and consumerism, it is very difficult to see how our ideas of what is 'good' might be tarnished by our assumptions about money.

Many churches today are far more sensitive to sexual sin than to financial sin, to the extent that they rarely think about the latter. Christians who refuse to see the wrong in adultery or pornography may eventually find themselves expelled from their churches, while those whose greed and gluttony is obvious to everyone will be tolerated, especially if they give generously to support the church. The reason is easy to understand. It is true that sexual sin is often easier to identify but the main reason is that financial sin is too close to home and too commonplace. And to challenge it risks the church's own financial stability!

To be a Christian means more than believing certain eternal truths, although this is the place to start. It means more than repentance for sin, which is a necessary step. We talk of new Christians as having 'been converted', but that is only a beginning. Christian salvation is a process that continues for the rest of a Christian's life, a progression that we can hasten or slow by our behaviour. This process is not the result of a new commitment but of new life: of being 'born again'. The original of the term 'born again' is from the English translation of a conversation Jesus had with Nicodemus, recorded in John 3, but the Greek words Jesus used really mean 'born from above'.

Nicodemus was one of the leading religious teachers in Israel. He had seen Jesus rise to prominence and probably heard how he turned water into wine at a wedding feast in Cana. He would certainly have known how Jesus chased the traders and bankers out of the Temple forecourt. Nicodemus visited Jesus in the night but I doubt this was because he was afraid of being seen with someone so controversial. I think it was too early in Jesus' career for that to worry a man like Nicodemus.

Jewish rabbis and scholars had a habit of discussing religious matters into the night and when Nicodemus addressed Jesus as rabbi, he signalled not only respect but also a serious concern to understand Jesus and his theology. Nicodemus opened the conversation by affirming that nobody could do what Jesus had done 'unless God is with him'. I expect he was referring not only to the supernatural power necessary to perform miracles but also to the sheer audacity and charisma needed to clear the Temple marketplace without being lynched!

Jesus cut into the conversation, getting straight to the core of Nicodemus' concern. 'Truly, truly, I say to you, unless one is born again he cannot see the Kingdom of God'. The word 'truly' is the same word often translated as 'amen', the word we say at the end of a prayer to signify that we agree with it. To say 'truly, truly', or 'amen, amen' at the start of a sentence was to emphasise the certainty of what you are going to say. Later in the conversation, Jesus told Nicodemus, 'Truly, truly, I say to you, we speak of what we know, and bear witness to what we have seen...'

Not surprisingly, the concept of a second birth perplexed Nicodemus. 'How can a man be born when he is old?' he asked. 'Can he enter a second time into his mother's womb and be born?' Jesus therefore clarified his point. 'Truly, truly, I say to you, unless one is born of water and the Spirit, he cannot enter the Kingdom of God. That which is born of the flesh is flesh, and that which is born of the Spirit is spirit.'

Nicodemus needed a second birth, a spiritual birth 'from above' in order to understand Jesus and his mission. Jesus then explained how it could happen. 'Do not marvel that I said to you, you must be born again. The wind blows where it wishes, and you hear its sound, but you do not know where it comes from or where it goes. So is everyone who is born of the Spirit.'

I can imagine the two men sitting on the roof of a house, enjoying a cool breeze after a hot day. Perhaps they could hear it whirring and whistling and stirring the trees. Today we know that changes in air pressure create wind and we can often predict its path but that does not at all detract from the imagery Jesus used, comparing it to the activity of the Holy Spirit. But like all the metaphors that Jesus used, we cannot press this one too far. Jesus went on to explain to Nicodemus that the action of the Holy Spirit is not as random as the path of the wind seemed to be. He also said that everyone who believes will be saved. He summed up the point in what has become the most famous quotation from the entire Bible: John 3:16-17.

For God so loved the world, that he gave his only Son, that whoever believes in him should not perish but have everlasting life. For God did not send his Son into the world to condemn the world, but in order that the world might be saved through him.

As there is no punctuation in the Greek language used in the New Testament, it is impossible to know where in this passage in John 3 the author stops quoting Jesus and begins to elaborate on what Jesus said. But it really does not make much difference. Whether Jesus stated the truth or John inferred it, it is true. Those who believe on Jesus will be saved. The question is, then, *What is it that we need to believe?*

I do not wish to make this more complicated than it is but it is worth recalling James' words that believing in God is not enough to be Christian. 'You believe that God is one; you do well', he wrote, but then added, 'Even the demons believe — and shudder!' (James 2:19). Some of the demons whom Jesus encountered knew that he was the Son of God, Israel's Messiah, but they were not pleased about it. They persisted in their rebellion and submitted to Jesus' authority only when left with no choice! That is not the sort of belief necessary for the new birth that Jesus described.

Again and again in the New Testament, we read the word 'repent'. 'Repent, for the Kingdom of Heaven is at hand!' was the basic messaged preached by John the Baptist and by Jesus. When Jesus sent his disciples out in pairs, it was with the message that people should repent. The preaching recorded in the Acts of the Apostles emphasises the same essential message, 'Repent therefore and be converted, that your sins may be blotted out…' (See, for example, Matthew 3:1-2, 4:17, Mark 6:7-13 and Acts 2:36-39)

To repent is to change your mind about something but it is more than academic, intellectual change. It is not like changing your mind about some fact in history that has little or no impact on the way you live. It is to change your mind about things as basic as how the world works and how we should live in it. We must acknowledge our sinful nature. This is not the same as acknowledging that we have done some wrong things in our life: every honest person will admit that. It is more fundamental. It is acknowledging the fact of a nature and attitude that is in rebellion against the LORD God.

It is in this quality of repentance that we acknowledge Jesus of Nazareth as the Christ, the Messiah or Saviour, and as God's Son who came to destroy the works of the devil and save people from sin. But even this belief is still a step short. We need not only to accept who Jesus is but also to commit ourselves to him by faith. By this, we enter a faith relationship with Jesus.

This is not to imply that by believing we make our own second birth happen. Rather, when we believe, the Holy Spirit implants inside us the new life. The Holy Spirit is a person with a will, not a force of nature like the wind, and he implants new life in believers.

We are not saved by perceiving our sin or understanding who Jesus is; we are not saved by grasping the mystery of Jesus' death and resurrection. Even grasping the mystery of how the Spirit comes into us with spiritual life does not save us. We are saved by yielding to the Lord Jesus Christ and, in our yielding, the Holy Spirit gives us new life and we are born again.

Jesus likened the Holy Spirit to the wind, so imagine that you are on a yacht. To sail, you need to believe that the wind will carry you over the water. Acting on that belief, you erect the sail. Your action does not make the yacht move but you have faith that, sooner or later, the wind will come and catch the sail and carry you along.

And when the wind does come, you do move. Our repentance, our belief in Jesus and our commitment to him is like hoisting the sail. As the Holy Spirit is a person, we can pray for him to make us born again, born from above, with spiritual life.

To be born again is to receive another life at the centre of our being, where the Holy Spirit implants something altogether new and different from what we received at our physical conception. Paul wrote that 'If anyone is in Christ, he is a new creation. The old has passed away; behold, the new has come' (2 Corinthians 5:17). This 'newness' is not complete and may not be immediately manifested in a person's life but it begins to grow and to make a difference. We should not try to detect new life by looking within ourselves, trying to identify the seed of life and observe its growth. Instead, we shall see the signs of life when it begins to make a difference in us. The new life makes us more alert to spiritual things, more discriminating about the way we live. But even this is still just the start.

Paul also wrote, 'Do not be conformed to this world, but be transformed by the renewal of your mind, that by testing you may discern what is the will of God, what is good and acceptable and perfect' (Romans 12:2). The new birth is the start of this renewing but it is a process that we need to cooperate with and persist in seeing through. And there is still more.

A living organism is never an end in itself, never living for itself only. It has a larger purpose. The object of all life is to reproduce new life and that process is always sacrificial. In the plant world, death is often the only way to increase.

I suspect that the Parables of the Sower were Jesus' favourite stories for explaining both his central message and his method for spreading it. Jesus described the process again when he said, 'Truly, truly, I say to you, unless a grain of wheat falls into the earth and dies, it remains alone; but if it dies, it bears much fruit. Whoever loves his life loses it, and whoever hates his life in this world will keep it for eternal life. If anyone serves me, he must follow me; and where I am, there will my servant be also. If anyone serves me, the Father will honour him' (John 12:24-26).

The life in a grain of wheat is barren unless it goes into the ground, where it begins to disintegrate. As it falls apart, losing its own shape and form, gradually something new sprouts and grows. In time, it breaks through the surface of the earth; in time, it forms a head that contains many more grains of wheat, each with its own life. Each new life seed has the life of the original grain and when those grains go back into the earth, the process is multiplied.

The life of God is in Jesus and it was not his birth or his teaching (as important as they are) but his death that made it possible for that life to spread. It is no different for his followers today. When Jesus met his disciples after his resurrection, he told them, 'As the Father has sent me, even so I am sending you' (John 20:21). To spread the good news of Jesus we have to die because Jesus' way is the way of all Christians.

Jesus died to spread the seed of spiritual life and Christians themselves die and live to spread more seed, all of it containing the life of Jesus. Christians respond to the call to be Jesus' disciples. There is more to being a disciple than there is to being a pupil or student: to live as a disciple is to forsake our own lifestyle, to 'die' to it, and to adopt the teacher's lifestyle. We see this in the Gospels, where Jesus' closest disciples were repeatedly out of step with him. They criticised the women who anointed Jesus with perfume, they wanted to call down judgment fire on the towns that rejected him and they thought the coming of the Kingdom of God meant the immediate end of Roman rule. They did not want Jesus to go to Jerusalem to die. Repeatedly, they had to adjust and adopt Jesus' ways of thinking and cooperate with what he was doing.

But this sort of dying to self is not at all the way of the consumer societies in which most of us live, where thorns easily choke us. The cares of the world includes the money we need to pay bills and access entertainment, to enjoy what everyone else seems to be enjoying and to fund a lifestyle that will show others how well we are doing. The deceitfulness of riches would try to persuade us that, although money cannot buy us happiness, we would be a little happier with just a little more than we have already. (The fact is, in as much as it is possible to evaluate these things, the more surplus money people have the more burdened and less happy they are!) The desires for other things, the cares and the pleasures of life, the need to accumulate money and possessions, the struggling for relief from the pressures of life, the striving for novelty to relieve monotony: these things may not choke spiritual life to the point of death but they prevent growth towards Christian maturity.

When Jesus mentioned the Kingdom of God, he got to the heart of Nicodemus' concern. Every Israelite at the time knew the phrases, 'Kingdom of God' and 'Kingdom of Heaven'. Although they had no comprehensive idea of precisely what they meant, they assumed the restoration of Israel as a fully independent nation would be included. This often presupposed the overthrow of Roman rule, something many assumed the Messiah would achieve, and Jesus' disciples believed this. In fact, they did not finally shake off the belief until after Jesus had ascended back to heaven.

The Kingdom is a work in progress. When applied to human affairs, a kingdom usually indicates established authority but Peter explains that Jesus 'must reign *until* he has put all his enemies under his feet', at which point he hands it over to his father (1 Corinthians 15:24-25).

The Kingdom is God's rule through intimacy. Although God is sovereign, and his power extends over all of creation, from the highest heaven to the deepest hell, the Kingdom is a narrower sphere of influence: it is where God's will is done on earth as it is in Heaven, in loving cooperation by people who are devoted to him.

Unlike the kingdoms of the world, the Kingdom of God is eternal and a place of love, peace, forgiveness and spiritual values. The particular skills that its citizens need to live include words of wisdom and knowledge, faith, healing and miracles, prophecy, discerning spiritual influences, speaking and interpreting mysterious languages (tongues). Its 'gross national product' is measured in fruit such as love, joy, peace, longsuffering, kindness, goodness, faithfulness, gentleness and self-control. Its 'exports' are peace on earth and goodwill to all people!

In the Kingdom, the first shall be last, the poor and those who suffer are blessed, the meek inherit the earth and the humble are exalted. It is where the leaders are those who serve. It is where we are to 'turn the other cheek' to those who abuse us and do good to our enemies. The devotional and charitable actions done in secret are openly rewarded by God but the ones done 'to be seen' by people are (at best) of temporal advantage only. Money given to the poor buys incorruptible treasure in heaven but the treasures hoarded on earth are lost to theft and decay. Victory comes out of perceived defeat: this is the way of the cross!

The Kingdom of God is so very different from the way human societies function that something as radical and supernatural as new birth is necessary to see and enter into it. It follows that Christians who see themselves as citizens of the Kingdom should not use money like everyone else: it is not simply unnecessary but contrary to how life should be lived in dependence on God.

If you plant a single grain of wheat in a field, it is possible it could multiply year after year and eventually fill the entire field with a tremendous harvest. If you plant a gold coin in the field, after a 100 years or 1,000 years it will still be a single gold coin. Its value may have increased as it became rarer but it could never reproduce.

Money is not the root of all evil, although many people suppose it is because Paul is very often misquoted. The *love of* money is the root. On one occasion, Jesus explained to some Pharisees that it is not what we take into ourselves that pollutes us but what springs out from our hearts. The occasion — or perhaps they are two similar occasions — is recorded in Matthew 23 and Luke 11. Although Jesus was talking about religious cleaning rituals, his words apply equally to our attitude to money. We may be scrupulously correct in the ways we get and use money but if the love of money is flowing from our hearts, the outward 'rituals' do us no good at all. Jesus exposed greed, self-indulgence and wickedness that lay beneath those Pharisees' scrupulous veneer!

With this in mind, take some time to examine your own lifestyle. Is the environment in which you live and work choking the Word of God and your spiritual growth? Could your outward conformity to legal and ethical standards mask an inner avarice?

The only way to know this is to start to track all the money you spend. List the payment of every bill; list every chocolate bar, magazine, coffee and snack you buy. List the cost of your food and fuel and clothes. And list your regular giving and the occasional coins you drop into charity boxes. Record the purpose of every single penny or cent you part with. Then sort your spending into these categories:

Essentials. These are the things that you cannot avoid paying for and they will depend on your personal situation. They will almost certainly include rent or mortgage, water, food, basic clothes, fuel (perhaps electricity or gas), personal hygiene (soap, toothpaste, kitchen cleaners and the rest) and medication. They will probably include essential transport and communication (like mobile, telephone and internet access), national and local taxes. They will include all insurance that you are required by law to have (such as for motoring) or to cover loss you could not expect to pay for from savings (like house insurance).

List separately under this heading any overdue bills you are repaying and any loans or other credit repayments for costs that you could not pay outright.

Conveniences. These things are not essential but they make life easier for you. They include some household equipment and gadgets. They might also include things like meals and snacks you purchased because it was easier for you than preparing a meal when you get home, perhaps at the end of a very long day at work or because of some other time constraint.

Include any loans and other credit repayments for lifestyle costs you incurred in the past but are still paying for. Include any insurance premiums that are not included under Essentials.

Pleasures. Include here leisure activities, entertainments and hobbies. These things are not unimportant but they are not *essential* to maintaining our homes and staying healthy. We all need a social life and in some parts of the world it is almost impossible to meet people without paying for transport and to go places together. Again, include any loans and credit repayments for these things that you bought in the past but have not finished paying for, like the cost of a party, a television, theatre tickets, restaurant meals or music downloads.

List separately under this heading your impulse spending. By that, I mean the things you buy without really thinking. Drinks, sweets, snacks, newspapers and magazines, music and videos and anything else that catches your eye in a shop or on the internet that you did not want before you saw it but bought immediately.

Saving. This includes all savings and investments, whether you are saving for something specific, like Christmas or a holiday, or as a sensible precaution in case things go wrong or need replacing in the future. (The difference between savings and investments is often blurred today but, put simply, savings are money stored as safely as possible, without much concern for how much it may increase with interest, while investments are made with the primary intention of making more money and therefore with a greater risk of loss.)

Giving. This includes giving to a church or charity or to any good cause or worthy person, expecting nothing — nothing at all! — in return.

It is important that you know where your money is going. If you are embarrassed by what you discover about yourself, you do not have to share the information with anyone else. But do not think that ignorance or self-denial are better options! This self-knowledge is what people must learn if they are to take control of their money when struggling to make ends meet or already in debt. But there is a deeper reason for doing it, even if your income comfortably exceeds all your outgoings and you are generous in helping others with what you have left over.

Tracking every penny or cent we spend helps to bring alive to us the reality of our own lifestyle values, especially those of us who live in consumer societies. It reveals our true priorities and shows the gap between who we think we are and the person we actually are. If we think we are generous with our money, we may find that we spend far more on our own convenience and pleasure than helping others pay for their essentials.

Tracking our spending also shows the gap between the sort of person we are and who we ought to be as disciples of Jesus of Nazareth. It can alert us to when we held back from helping someone — from loving our neighbour as ourselves — because of the financial cost involved. It can show how entwined we are among the thorns, how the spiritual life is being choked out of us. It can therefore point the way to spiritual growth and maturity!

This raises a final issue that is not easy to decide or give advice about. Just what, if anything, do we need to give up or give away? If we are not the sort of people who are like Zacchaeus, who need to make restitution to people we have cheated, how do we know if we are the sorts of people who need to do what the rich young ruler could not bring himself to do, to give away all our wealth?

A helpful place to start thinking about this is to liken ourselves to sailors on a ship loaded with goods. To prevent ships from being overloaded, plimsoll lines are drawn around the outside of their hulls. If the line goes beneath the water, the cargo is too heavy for the ship to be safe. But sometimes a modestly loaded ship can get into a terrible storm and the crew have to throw its cargo overboard to stay safe. Given the choice, the crew would rather reach port without their cargo than die trying to hold on to it.

You could conclude from this that we should develop the skill of knowing just when to ditch 'cargo' that threatens our spiritual survival. But, unlike sailors who need to get as much of their cargo as possible to port, we are free to ditch as much as we like. When Paul wrote to the church at Philippi, he explained that he counted everything as loss for the excellency of knowing Jesus Christ (Philippians 3). He was not therefore disturbed when he lost things, for he already thought of them as loss. Moreover, in Christ he had infinite gain. He was not a sailor escaping shipwreck with nothing but his life but a Christian going forward to his reward in heaven.

We should be more like Paul. We need not aspire to poverty, discomfort and poor health in the pursuit of spiritual gain but it is the case that the more we aspire to be faithful disciples of Jesus Christ of Nazareth, the less burdened we will want to be with unnecessary materialism.

3: Be on your guard against all covetousness

Take care, and be on your guard against all covetousness, for one's life does not consist in the abundance of his possessions.
Luke 12:15

AVARICE AND COVETOUSNESS are often treated as the same thing but that is not entirely accurate. The Hebrew and Greek words for covet used in the Bible mean to desire, to set our hearts on something and to long for it. Avarice used to be described as coveting money but that fails to convey adequately the force of avarice and the completeness with which it can take over a personality.

While covetousness is desire, avarice is a cosmology; while covetousness is (as Paul observed) the sin of idolatry, avarice is a way of looking at the whole of life and trying to make it work for you on our own terms.

There is a difference between a coin collector coveting a particular coin because of its beauty, rarity or historical significance and someone who wants money for what it can achieve, for the independence, possessions and influence it can buy them.

At the heart of sin is an attitude that says, 'I want to be like God; I want to be my own god. I want to run my own life, to have my own way. I want to meet my own needs and fulfil my own dreams'. That is why John could write with simplicity that, 'Sin is lawlessness', because it is living outside God's remit and provision. That attitude has been bred into the human race through the centuries and money is what people rely on to fulfil their needs and ambitions when they do not rely on God.

When we cut ourselves off from God, from the source of God's love and seek to make our own way, we really have no choice but to take what we can get to survive and succeed. What begins as a natural desire to survive soon develops into an inordinate desire to succeed and, often, to succeed at *any* cost. We accumulate food, clothes, shelter, self-worth and status for ourselves. And most of all, we accumulate money because that is often the means to getting all the rest.

Instead of loving others, we began to drain them and even plunder our most intimate relationships. We begin to neglect and use our families and friends for our own fulfilment, only giving out if we already have plenty. Some people eventually come to realise this, like the retiring businesspeople who wish they had spent more time with their families. When our personalities are corrupted in this way, we have not only the urge of sin but also a personality that can only sin.

When our security and self-worth come from our job, home, car, investment portfolio or social standing, we can feed our egos only by taking from others. But if our identity, significance and security comes from the God who created us, and if our sense of purpose is what God wants us to do here on earth, and if we are confident in God's willingness to care for us, we can affirm people for their own worth and love our neighbours as ourselves.

This is why coveting is forbidden in the last of the Ten Commandments, acting like a gatekeeper to the murder, adultery, theft and other offences against God forbidden in the previous commandments. As the very essence of coveting is temptation, it is the most natural sin to overlook or excuse and I think this is why Paul wrote that if it had not been for the Law he would never have known what coveting is: he would not have thought it sin if it were not specifically forbidden. The Tenth Commandment therefore acted as a 'straight edge' or plumb line to show up crookedness he might not otherwise have noticed in himself.

I think another reason why the Ten Commandments end by forbidding coveting is that it is a prohibition on selfishness and therefore states negatively the same thing as the commandment to love our neighbours as ourselves. If we covet, we love ourselves inordinately! If we love our neighbours *as ourselves*, we will not covet but want to help them with the things they need and that are important to them. I expect this is why Jesus, when he told the rich young ruler about keeping the commandments, did not end with the one about not coveting but, positively, with the need to love others (Matthew 19:19).

Jesus' warning against covetousness is, I think, one that most Christians would accept as being right and necessary in a very general sort of way. Be on your guard against covetousness, beware of wanting things and of wanting them so much that just wanting becomes an addiction! But when we understand the examples of coveting in the Hebrew Scriptures, and realise the context in which Jesus gave his warning, it suddenly becomes unsettling and challenging. I believe the extent of our own covetousness will amaze us.

* * *

The background to what Jesus of Nazareth said about coveting is traced from the Ten Commandments when, for the first time, desiring things was forbidden. This version is in Exodus 20:17.

> You shall not covet your neighbour's house; you shall not covet your neighbour's wife, or his male servant, or his female servant, or his ox, or his donkey, or anything that is your neighbour's.

The version that appears in Deuteronomy 5 reverses the order of the first two things forbidden, beginning with a neighbour's wife, and also includes a neighbour's field. I expect Moses made the changes to take account of how different things would be in the Promised Land, where most people would for the first time in Israel's history have homes built on their own land. I think the difference also emphasises the essential flexibility of the Law: not legislation to be studied for loopholes but lifestyle guidance to be embraced and adapted to personal situations.

The prohibition on coveting was never limited to coveting the possessions of the people who lived nearby. If the Israelites had remembered this, they may not have been tempted to join in the pagan festivities of neighbouring communities. Today, it would embrace everything we see in shops, in magazines, at the cinema and on television. If that temptation were not enough to resist, the relentless marketing, advertising and sales talk that fuel consumerism purposefully exploit coveting, generating dissatisfaction and promoting insatiability. All this creates the illusion that it is not only natural but also good to want more, more and still more things.

The Hebrew Scriptures contain some devastating examples of coveting. When Joshua prepared the Israelite army to take the city of Jericho, he passed on to them God's prohibition not to take anything for themselves from the city. It was the practice in the ancient world that the soldiers in conquering armies could plunder the people they conquered but God forbade this at Jericho. Certain valuable things were to go into the treasury, to be used for the good of *all* the people, and all the rest was to be destroyed (Joshua 6:17-19).

One man, Achan, did not obey this prohibition. He kept some things for himself. It is interesting how this is described at the start of Joshua 7: 'But the *people of Israel* broke faith in regard to the devoted things, *for Achan*...took some of the devoted things. And the anger of the LORD burned *against the people of Israel*.' Did just one man's greed taint the whole nation? I think we can infer that other people saw Achan take plunder for himself. Perhaps these were the soldiers with him in the defeated city or his neighbours who saw him acting suspiciously on his return to the camp. Almost certainly, his family knew.

When Achan was found out, he explained what had happened like this. 'Truly I have sinned against the LORD God of Israel, and this is what I did: when I saw among the spoil a beautiful cloak from Shinar and two hundred shekels of silver, and a bar of gold weighing fifty shekels, then I coveted them and took them.'

Shinar was a city on the plain of Babylon and the cloak would have been distinctive. The silver was probably silver rings or jewellery but, at the time, only Babylon was known to store gold as bars. It was a very valuable find.

Achan coveted and kept this forbidden wealth. He might easily have rationalised his greed by thinking that he deserved to keep it, as a solider in any other army would have been allowed to keep it. But he was not in any other army but serving the living

God. Most of the things he took should have been put into the treasury, for *everyone's* benefit, and so I wonder if he perhaps thought the same sort of thoughts that persuade people today — including, in my experience, some Christians — to fiddle their taxes. Often, their self-justification is that 'everybody does it'!

The most notorious example of coveting in the Old Testament is King Ahab. Although history remembers him as one of Israel's great rulers, because he enlarged the kingdom, secured its borders and increased trade with the surrounding nations, the Bible describes him as Israel's most wicked king. Some of his successors may have behaved even more wickedly but Ahab set the trend by marrying a foreign princess, worshipping foreign gods and exploiting his own people.

Ahab's neighbour, Naboth, had a vineyard that Ahab wanted to turn into a vegetable garden: the story is recorded in 1 Kings 21. Ahab made a generous offer to buy the vineyard but Naboth refused. I suppose Naboth might have been prepared to lease the vineyard if the King had wanted it as a vineyard but the King had no intention of preserving it. He wanted to consume it, turning it into a vegetable garden. And he wanted to do that for no better reason than it was convenient for him, next to where he lived.

Naboth looked on his family property as something he kept in trust for future generations 'The LORD forbid that I should give you the inheritance of my fathers', he told the King.

The King retreated into his house to sulk, which is where his wife found him. Queen Jezebel had been bought up in a country where the royal family was used to getting its own way. She arranged for Naboth to be falsely accused of blasphemy, a crime that was punished by being stoned to death. After Naboth's execution, Ahab took possession of the vineyard but his enjoyment lasted only until the prophet Elijah visited with a message of judgement from God.

We should beware of coveting for no better reason than convenience. Some conveniences are properly justified. In some places, a car can be much more convenient than using public transport and so there are good reasons to have one. Or two cars, perhaps, for large families or those living in remote places. Washing machines and fridges make life very much easier for families around the world. Businesspeople and office workers find life very much easier using computers; farmers and factory workers use equipment to do monotonous or complex tasks more quickly. Meals bought late at night on the way home from work at the end of a long day may be much more convenient than having to prepare them at home and then tidying up before resting. But King Ahab, with all his great wealth, did not need to destroy a vineyard that had been passed down from generation to generation *just* so he could have a vegetable garden nearby.

A third example of coveting is Gehazi, the prophet Elisha's servant. In 2 Kings 5, we read how Naaman, the military commander in Syria, went to Israel looking for a cure for his leprosy. He went because an Israelite servant had told him of a prophet who could cure him and, as unlikely as the story must have sounded, he was desperate enough to go.

Naaman went first to see Israel's king but he thought the request a political scam to provoke a war. When Elisha heard about this, he sent a message to the king and Naaman was directed to Elisha's home.

The prophet told Naaman that if he bathed seven times in the River Jordan he would be healed. At first, Naaman despised Elisha's prophecy but he was persuaded to test it and was healed. The miracle converted Naaman from his pagan religion to worship the LORD God. In gratitude, Naaman offered Elisha considerable wealth but Elisha refused it all. I expect that Elisha thought as Abraham had done before him, not wanting any individual person to be able to boast that he had made him rich (see Genesis14:21-24). I expect, too, that knowing God now had a faithful worshipper at the heart of the Syrian government was more valuable to Elisha than any amount material wealth. But Gehazi did not think the same way!

Soon after Naaman had left to return home to Syria, Gehazi chased after him and said that Elisha had changed his mind and wanted silver and clothing to give to some young men. Gehazi lied but Naaman gave gladly more than what was asked and assigned two men to escort Gehazi home. Gehazi had not been greedy: I expect the two men sent with him were more for protection from bandits than to bear the load. God revealed the lie to Elisha. When challenged, Gehazi tried to cover up with more lies but he was punished by God with Naaman's leprosy.

Although what Gehazi asked for was modest, the sin of coveting is not in wanting much but in wanting anything that God has not provided. I therefore think it is probably a mistake when Bibles use the word 'greed' instead of 'covet', because greed implies wanting a lot.

Gehazi's desire to benefit from Elisha's prophetic gift takes us back a few hundred years, to a time before Joshua led the people into the land that would become Israel, to the story of Balaam. As we saw in the last chapter, Balaam has gone down in history as the man who wanted to make money out of his relationship with God and the supernatural gift that God had given him. He might have served God gloriously if he had not 'loved gain from wrongdoing' (2 Peter 2:15). His story is told in Numbers 22-24.

King Balak of Moab had watched the Israelites journey around the wilderness towards their Promised Land and he knew that with God behind them they would be invulnerable. Balak's people were 'overcome with fear' and so he sent messengers to Balaam to ask him to curse the Israelites. Like Naaman's plan to find a miracle cure for leprosy, Balak's plan may seem fanciful but Balaam's reputation for pronouncing both curses and blessings was well known. There is no doubt that Balaam was in touch with God!

When Balak's messengers arrived, Balaam should have sent them away as soon as he heard what they wanted him to do. He could not seriously think that God would allow his own chosen people to be cursed! Instead, Balaam asked God what to do. I think there are times when we do not need to ask God what to do because his will is so obvious. As expected, God forbade Balaam to go to Balak.

When King Balak sent a second, more impressive group of messengers to Balaam, with the promise of still greater rewards for cursing the Israelites, rather than simply sending them away Balaam decided to see if God had changed his mind. Surprisingly, God seems to have done just that. 'If the men have come to call you, rise, go with them', he told Balaam, 'but only do what I tell you.'

Balaam went with the King's messengers. Jumping to near the end of the story, we find that three times Balaam tried to curse the Israelites but each time heard himself blessing them. This seriously upset King Balak but, as we discover, Balaam nevertheless found a way to help Balak undermine the Israelites and earn the King's reward.

In Numbers 25, we read how the young women in Moab invited the Israelites to their pagan festivals, where they joined in the worship of Baal. We read in Revelation 2:14 that this was done on Balaam's advice. This brought God's judgement on the Israelites and, as a result, at least 24,000 of them died. (Incidentally, Balaam died in battle later on.)

The New Testament contains a tragic example of how subtle coveting can be. We have already seen how Barnabas sold some land and gave the proceeds to help people in need. We then read in Acts 5 how husband and wife, Ananias and Sapphira, copied his example. Tragically, they lied when they said that they had donated *all* the proceeds of the sale because they kept some of it for themselves. Why did they keep some back? Perhaps one or both of them felt the need to retain some of the money in case of need in the future. Keeping back some of the money was not, however, the problem: their lie was the problem! Was it to cover up their lack of faith? If so, they should not have been afraid to admit it because we are all liable to experience doubts about what action to take. Did they lie to enhance their status in the church? I think they did! Ananias gave the gift to the apostles *publicly*, probably in the course of worship; later, Sapphira lied about the extent of their generosity to the apostles, again *in public*. I think they coveted the sort of recognition that Barnabas had. If that is right, they had forgotten that Barnabas was highly regarded because he was a great encourager and not because of a single act of generosity, even though generosity was important in the early church.

These examples of coveting show how it can corrupt anyone, even someone with as much wealth and power as King Ahab, and even someone as involved with the one true God as Balaam, Gehazi, Ananias and Sapphira. But Jesus' warning about coveting exposes much deeper flaws in our characters! The account of how Jesus came to give the warning is recorded in Luke 11:37-12:59 and by looking at the sequence of events that day we can see the dangers.

After a confrontation with some Pharisees, Jesus was accused of being in league with the devil! Then, surprisingly, one of the Pharisees invited him to dinner. Possibly exhausted, Jesus reclined at the table without first washing his feet. This astonished the host and Jesus used the opportunity to compare ritual cleanliness with authentic righteousness. And he criticised the Pharisees' self-aggrandisement. This insulted the other guests. It seems that Jesus left without eating anything and was pursued by a group of agitators, trying to provoke him into further argument.

This drew a crowd of many thousands and the situation began to get dangerous: 'they were trampling one another'! Jesus warned the crowd about the Pharisees' hypocrisy, encouraged them to trust in God and then described his mission as a direct rebuke to those who had accused him of working with the devil. Then, from the crowd, a man shouted, 'Teacher, tell my brother to divide the inheritance with me'.

What provoked the man to ask such a question? While the Jews at that time often went to religious teachers to resolve such issues, this was hardly the time or the place! Was the question another set up by the Pharisees, designed to trap Jesus? I expect it was and that is why, amidst the pandemonium, Jesus had the opportunity to answer. Before we hear his response, we need to consider the problem.

In Israel at the time, a father whose eldest child was a son was expected to leave that son a double portion of his estate: that is, twice as much as each of his younger brothers. (Daughters did not receive anything unless they had no brothers.) The case presented to Jesus seems to have involved just two brothers, so the elder would have received two-thirds of their father's estate and the younger one third. I think we can assume that the man who appealed to Jesus had been disinherited entirely, although it is possible that he wanted Jesus to propose a more advantageous division, giving him half of the estate. Either way, Jesus' reply was stunning!

Even though the case may have been a genuine one, some Pharisees could have told the man to put it to Jesus as a test. I think this may be why Jesus declared himself to be above such quarrels. 'Man', he said, 'who made me a judge or arbitrator over you?' But then he went further, to expose the greed that motivated the question. 'Take care, and be on your guard against all covetousness, for one's life does not consist in the abundance of his possessions'. We should be startled by that! Whether the man wanted justice or fairness, Jesus called it covetousness!

Jesus pressed home his point with a parable about a fortunate farmer who has become known as 'the rich fool'. Getting a bumper harvest, the farmer thought to himself, 'What shall I do, for I have nowhere to store my crops?' Then he had an idea! 'I will do this: I will tear down my barns and build larger ones, and there I will store all my grain and my goods'. The purpose of this was entirely selfish. 'Soul' he said to himself, 'you have ample goods laid up for many years; relax, eat, drink, be merry.'

No doubt, the fortunate farmer was skilful and diligent but he must have realised that his bumper harvest was not simply the result of his own hard work. As a farmer, he could not have underestimated the role of nature in his success; as a Jew, he should have attributed that success to God. Perhaps he did realise these things but, if he did, he did not act accordingly.

Had the fortunate farmer acted consistent with his belief, he would have shared his good fortune for the benefit of the entire community. He might have legitimately sold the excess harvest, the abundance reducing the price for his customers while still making for himself a nice profit. Proverbs 11:26 says, 'The people curse him who holds back grain, but a blessing is on the head of him who sells it'. The use of the word 'sells' is significant: there was nothing odious in selling the excess for profit. The farmer's foolishness was not that he failed to give away the abundant harvest, although giving it away would have been better and he would have accumulated treasure in heaven, but that he hoarded it.

Today, we may find it difficult to see how wanting our legal entitlement to an inheritance or keeping the proceeds of our own hard work is covetous but it is something that James criticised rich Christians for in James 5:1-5.

Come now, you rich, weep and howl for the miseries that are coming upon you. Your riches have rotted and your garments are moth-eaten. Your gold and silver have corroded, and their corrosion will be evidence against you and will eat your flesh like fire. You have laid up [literally, hoarded] treasure in the last days. Behold, the wages of the labourers who mowed your fields, which you kept back by fraud, are crying out against you, and the cries of the harvesters have reached the ears of the Lord of hosts.

I expect neither these Christians nor the fortunate farmer needed what they hoarded. The case of the disinherited man is equivocal but there is nothing to suggest that he was poor, particularly if he was posing a hypothetical question on behalf of the religious establishment.

Luke 6 records a time when Jesus was talking about loving our enemies. He said this: 'Give to everyone who asks of you. *And from him who takes away your goods do not ask them back*'. We will consider giving to everyone who asks things of us in the next chapter but now we should consider whether Jesus really meant to say that Christians are not even to try to get back the goods that are taken from us. Did he mean to say that if someone steals our wallet or purse, hacks into our bank account, or steals our identity to get credit in our name, we should be content with our loss and make no effort to recover our possessions?

I do not think that Jesus was referring to crime but to persecution and, with that in mind, we should recall Jesus words at the start of the Sermon on the Mount. 'Blessed are those who are persecuted for righteousness' sake, for theirs is the kingdom of heaven. Blessed are you when others revile you and persecute you and utter all kinds of evil against you falsely on my account. Rejoice and be glad, *for your reward is great in heaven*, for so they persecuted the prophets who were before you.'

To believe that the value of spiritual wealth far exceeds material wealth is not idealistic piety. I have always found challenging the passage in Hebrews 6 where the readers are reminded of the persecution they had suffered in the past: '[You] joyfully accepted the plundering of your goods, knowing that you have a better and an enduring possession for yourselves in heaven' (Hebrews 10:34). I may be pragmatic in such circumstances but would I be *joyful*?

Returning to Jesus' confrontation with the Pharisees, he focused on his disciples and repeated part of his message in the Sermon on the Mount about worrying about everyday necessities like food and clothing and the confidence they could have in God's desire to provide for them. He then told them to live with a prevailing sense of expectation.

Stay dressed for action and keep your lamps burning, and be like men who are waiting for their master to come home from the wedding feast, so that they may open the door to him at once when he comes and knocks. Blessed are those servants whom the master finds awake when he comes. Truly, I say to you, he will dress himself for service and have them recline at table, and he will come and serve them. If he comes in the second watch, or in the third, and finds them awake, blessed are those servants! But know this, that if the master of the house had known at what hour the thief was coming, he would not have left his house to be broken into. You also must be ready, for the Son of Man is coming at an hour you do not expect.

The image of having our waists girded and our lamps burning, ready to act on a moment's notice, is like firefighters or fighter pilots on standby, ready to go as soon as the alarm sounds. They do not have to finish what they were doing, think about what they need to take or check that their equipment is in order. They and everything they need is ready to go! That is how Christians should be, waiting for Jesus' return. I think this is why the letters preserved for us in the New Testament convey the sense that the writers thought that Jesus would return very soon, even though they knew that would not necessarily be the case.

What, then, does Jesus think when we ask him for things we do not need or are needless, gratuitous conveniences and pleasures? We know that when there is genuine need, we can rely on God to provide it, but what does he think when we want a 'fair share' that we do not actually need or compensation for an injustice that has not significantly disadvantaged us?

A temptation that Christians have always rationalised is that getting rich will enable them to do good things with the money. In the 4th Century, Evagrios the Solitary warned that the 'desire for wealth for giving to the poor' is 'another trick of the evil one'. In the 18th Century, Charles Finney spoke to Christians about the dangers of 'conforming to the world' in business practice in order to make money that could be used to spread the Gospel and advance the Kingdom of God. He wrote, 'A holy church, that would act on the principles of the Gospel, would spread the Gospel faster than all the money that ever was in New York, or ever will be'. I hear Christians say similar things today: justifying their desire to make money, they say their main desire is to help people.

A theology has evolved that takes further this religious avarice, distorting the Bible's basic teaching about prospering and prosperity. To prosper used to mean to be successful or to do well and seems to have derived from the idea of doing well on a trading expedition. That is the sense when it is used in many translations of the Bible. But in the past 50 years or so, as money has become increasingly important, 'to prosper' has taken on new connotations. It now usually means to be rich.

You might not be like Balaam, exploiting a spiritual gift for commercial gain, but it is very easy today to slip into thinking like the rest of society, that money is an indication of success, and therefore God wants all his faithful servants to be materially rich.

When John wrote a local church elder called Gaius, he began by saying, 'Beloved, I pray that all may *go well* with you and that you may be in good health, as it goes well with your soul' (3 John 1:2). Some translations put it like this: 'Beloved, I pray that you *may prosper* in all things and be in health, just as your soul prospers'. That sort of translation is fair enough *if* we remember that the *original* meaning of 'prosper' is *to do well*. After all, God does not want us to do badly! Even Christians who take a traditional vow of poverty only give up personal possessions and luxury: they do not take a vow of destitution!

In addition, we ought to remember that the promises of prosperity in the Bible are directed to communities, not to individuals, so that the wealth they enjoyed was to be worked, not hoarded. I have heard preachers explain that God wants his people to be rich like Abraham but he was a farmer and his wealth consisted of what he needed to keep working in order to keep on farming in order to care for his family and employees. This is not to suggest that Abraham did not store up resources for the future. Many years later, when Abraham's grandson, Jacob, sent his own sons to Egypt to buy food during a famine, they took the money (probably silver rings) they had saved.

Deuteronomy 28 is a good example of a promise of working wealth. God sets out comprehensively many blessings that he has for his people who are faithful to him. The list is impressive and they would be not only a blessing to the nation of Israel but a means of the Israelites blessing other nations also. But while the description of the blessings takes up the first 14 verses of Deuteronomy 28, the rest of the chapter, *another 54 verses*, describe the consequences of unfaithfulness!

I can find nothing in the Bible to suggest that God wants people to be materially rich in the ways we understand wealth today as hoarding possessions and accumulating excessive savings. There is nothing wrong with living in nice homes, dressing well, driving comfortable cars, enjoying a pleasant social life, taking holidays and having sensible savings for the future. But Paul saw that covetousness is idolatry and warned the Christians in Corinth to 'flee from idolatry' (Colossians 3:5 & 1 Corinthians 10:14).

Unfortunately, generations of Christians today have grown up with capitalism and consumerism as the social norms that it is very easy for us to conform to what everyone else takes for granted. We learn very early in life that money is the means to get what we need and want. We learn to rely on it, to lay aside our other values and principles in order to get it. Christians who start jobs for no better reason than that they see an opportunity to make a lot of money are motivated by no better incentive than the sin of avarice. Yet very few see this. And even some who do, believe they have no alternative but to behave like everyone else.

When a Christian or church believes God has called it to a special task, the usual first step is to see if they have enough money. If there is not enough, the provision of money is seen as confirmation of the call. This approach is as disloyal to God as the ancient Israelites who put Asherah trees or poles in their fields.

Asherah was a goddess of fertility. When the Israelites arrived in the Promised Land, many of the people already living there placed trees or poles dedicated to Asherah in their fields to attract her favour, in the hope of a good crop. Some of the Israelites copied this practice. Although Asherah never exceeded the LORD God in the Israelites' esteem, she divided their loyalties, just as money can divide the loyalties of Christians today. Preachers often tell us that God is more important than money, something that is impossible for any Christian to disagree with, but the problem is not that money might be more important but that we think it sufficiently important to divert our attention and compromise our allegiance.

Might those Israelites have thought of their Asherah poles as some Christians today think of good luck charms or harmless superstitions, like not walking under ladders? If they did, it would have been a dangerous complacency. While there may be no 'gods' called Mammon, and no demons called Avarice or Covetousness, there are idols that are thought to be responsible for our poverty or wealth, like Dedun (Celtic) and T'shai-shen (Chinese).

In Corinth, some Christians believed that while there was nothing but superstition to the idols and used this rationale to justify attending the feasts and festivals associated with them. I suspect they went for essentially business reasons, to network, but Paul told them that demons worked through the idols. 'What do I imply then? That ... an idol is anything? No, I imply that what pagans sacrifice they offer to demons and not to God' (1 Corinthians 10:19-20). He explained that Christians should not participate in anything to do with demons as to do so risked provoking God's jealousy.

Financial imperatives may seem more intellectually viable than traditional idol worship but, as we saw in Chapter 1, Revelation reveals the true nature of the global financial system called Babylon. By the time of its destruction, it had 'become a dwelling place for demons, a haunt for every unclean spirit, a haunt for every unclean bird, a haunt for every unclean and detestable beast'. In light of Paul's warning, many Christians may be, albeit unwittingly, collaborating with Mammon sufficiently to compromise their allegiance to God.

In the last chapter, I described how Jesus told Nicodemus that he had to be born again to see or enter the Kingdom of God. On another occasion, Jesus developed that metaphor when he told his disciples that unless they became as little children they could not enter the Kingdom. Similar accounts appear in three of the Gospels.

Matthew 18 begins with the disciples asking Jesus who will be greatest in the Kingdom of God. Jesus answered by calling a child to Himself and saying, 'Unless you are converted and become as little children you will by no means enter the Kingdom of Heaven'. Having been born again, or born from above with spiritual life, we must then grow as little children. Mark 9:33-37 and Luke 9:46-48 go into more detail. 'If anyone would be first, he must be last of all and servant of all' Jesus explained. He then picked up a child and added, 'Whoever receives one such child in my name receives me...' A little while later, recorded in Mark 10:13-16 and Luke 18:15-17, Jesus said, 'Let the little children come to me, for such is the Kingdom of God... Whoever does not receive the Kingdom of God as a little child will by no means enter it'.

Jesus was obviously talking about childlikeness, *not childishness*, and these three unsophisticated, uncomplicated childlike qualities are worth reflecting on.

Love without calculation. Children do not love in response to being fed and clothed by their parents but they simply have inside themselves the instinct to love. As they grow, they may learn to curb their love and use it to manipulate their parents, bartering it for rewards and affection, but, at the start, their love is natural, unfeigned devotion and emotion.

Disposition to learn. Although many children do not like the discipline of attending school, long before this they instinctively learn basic life skills from their parents. They learn to crawl, walk and run. They learn basic personal hygiene ('potty training'), how to feed and dress themselves — and how to work the television!

Straightforwardness of attitude. This is what previous generations would have called innocence but, unfortunately, today that quality has the connotation of being naïve and a bit foolish. Children quickly learn from adults to be calculating, cunning and crafty in the ways they present themselves and approach people. They may learn this at a very young age but it is contrary to the simple, candid way that children often say impulsively what they mean and mean without embarrassment what they say. Peter told his readers to lay aside all malice, deceit, hypocrisy, envy, and all evil speaking and as new-born babes to desire children's food, 'the pure spiritual milk, that by it you may grow up into salvation' (1 Peter 2:1-2).

To enter the Kingdom of God, we need to trust God instinctively, want to learn the skills for living there, even though these are not at all like the skills necessary for living in a capitalist, consumer society, and be straightforward with people.

Christian teachers have often described avarice and covetousness as 'deadly' sins. They were deadly because they could kill your soul, the real you, and kill your relationship with God. With this in mind, look again at how you spend money and ask yourself some uncomfortable questions about coveting. Keep in mind Achan, who may have thought that he could be like everyone else and did not fully appreciate his position as one of God's Chosen People. Remember also Gehazi, who did not covet much but squandered his unique position as servant to God's prophet.

Do you instinctively feel you have little choice but to maintain a lifestyle like your neighbours or work colleagues? Are you anxious for your children to have the same lifestyle accessories as their friends? Do you find yourself buying things that you hope will make you be, *or appear to be*, more capable, reliable, relaxed or happy?

A school teacher who was a Muslim told me that when she discovered her teenage son had bought lots of shirts, she had explained to him that it was a level of extravagance inappropriate to their family's situation. It was not that the family could not afford the clothes but that there was no need to buy so many or such quality. There were, she explained, more important things to spend their money on, including helping others less well off than themselves. It struck me that many Christian families might benefit from similar conversations.

The title of this book is, *Living with God and Money*, because we are to serve God but need to use money. We must therefore learn to *use*, not *serve*, money. We must resist the influence of the people around us who, to some degree, are pressurised by society and greed into earning more than they need, saving more than is necessary, spending to meet other people's perceptions and giving only what they will not miss to help others less fortunate.

When Paul warned Timothy about the love of money, he explained, 'There is great gain in godliness with contentment, for we brought nothing into the world, and we cannot take anything out of the world. But if we have food and clothing, with these we will be content.' (1 Timothy 6:6-7). Food and clothing — and by implication, shelter — are the basic survival needs for every human being but in certain cultures there are other essential costs. We looked at some of these in the last chapter. In addition, we spend money on the 'conveniences' that make life easier and 'pleasures' that help to make it enjoyable. But in many cultures, what we may think of as convenient is, in fact, extravagant, and our spending on pleasures can easily soon spiral out of control, especially living in consumer societies where many of the things and experiences we are encouraged to buy are designed to make us feel good for a few minutes only.

Some people think that on my courses I should give specific guidance about how much is reasonable for people to spend on conveniences and pleasures and how much to give to help others unable to enjoy those things. I refrain because everyone is different and, while it may be possible to point to specific cases of excess, we cannot really know what others need or the level of comfort and convenience appropriate to their situation. Some people, for example, may need to spend more than others on their clothes or on meals out because of their job. Some may need a better quality car than anyone else in their church, while others may need to travel first class or business class, perhaps because of a medical problem or the need to work with a degree of privacy on the journey.

In the Bible, Joseph and Daniel were senior statesmen who lived appropriate to their status but, it seems, without extravagance. Joseph seems to have cared well for his servants and was used to entertaining strangers; Daniel clearly thought the kings he served were decadent. Without a deep understanding of peoples' needs, we cannot judge their choices. All I can do here is to invite you to think about your own lifestyles and start to identify what is necessary, what is convenient and pleasurable — and what is excessive!

It is inevitable that some Christians will experience poverty. There can be very ordinary reasons for this, including a natural foolishness that fails to set proper spending priorities. More generally, we must never forget that Christians are not immune to the ramifications of living in a fallen and flawed world. All of us can catch colds, be involved in traffic accidents and fall down stairs. We all make mistakes but even the most prudent financial decisions can turn sour due to unforeseeable developments. Also, Christians can expect to experience God's discipline from time to time (Hebrews 12:3-17) and this may include financial pressures.

All I can say is that the more carefully we drive, the less likely we are to be involved in traffic accidents, and the better we handle money, the less likely it is that we will have financial problems. While we should take more care to avoid sinning than to avoid poverty, if we make good use of what we have and live according to God's standards, usually we can expect sufficient for our needs and enough to help others.

Agur ben Jakeh was a wise man in ancient Israel who collected proverbs and he preserved this prayer for our guidence (Proverbs 30:7-9).

> *Two things I ask of you;*
> *deny them not to me before I die:*
> *Remove far from me falsehood and lying;*
> *give me neither poverty nor riches;*
> *feed me with the food that is needful for me,*
> *lest I be full and deny you*
> *and say, 'Who is the LORD?'*
> *or lest I be poor and steal*
> *and profane the name of my God.*

Agur's prayer does not ask for a specific amount of money, a specific quantity or quality of food — or any other resource. It asks only for what is 'needful'. The Hebrew means more than essential and includes everything we should or ought to have: everything appropriate for our situation. This should be enough to keep us from deceit and dishonesty but not so much as to make us too satisfied and complacent, so that we might begin to delude ourselves that we are not utterly dependent upon God for everything. That is the contentment we should all strive for, irrespective of the prevailing views of society.

Paul described Jesus as 'the image of the invisible God' (Colossians 1:15). Even if the Bible told us nothing more about God we would see in Jesus how loving and generous he is. Jesus of Nazareth was always going out to other people, always loving and giving out. God made us to be outgoing: to share and give, not to accumulate and hoard. He created our personalities to enjoy the love we receive from him and to share it with others. We can safely give freely of ourselves and all that we have, knowing that God will supply our needs, as Jesus affirmed. We need not fear for what might happen in the future and have no need to covet.

4: It is more blessed to give than to receive

I coveted no one's silver or gold or apparel. You yourselves know that these hands ministered to my necessities and to those who were with me. In all things I have shown you that by working hard in this way we must help the weak and remember the words of the Lord Jesus, how he himself said, 'It is more blessed to give than to receive.'
Acts 20:33-35

THE ABOVE PASSAGE is the conclusion of Paul's farewell speech to the leaders of the church at Ephesus. He quotes words of Jesus that are not in any of the Gospels: 'It is more blessed to give than to receive.'

To be blessed is to be favoured. I think it fair to say that it means being lucky or fortunate, although without the connotation of coincidence or chance those words usually convey. It means to be happy and to prosper. But giving, not accumulating, is the route to this prosperity.

A Christian lifestyle entails more than an absence of covetousness but an attitude that runs in the very opposite direction. But this sort of life can be lived only by relying on God, not on money, particularly in a society where accumulation is expected and respected.

Psalm 112 describes the blessings enjoyed by people who fear the LORD and delight in his commandments. They include, 'He has distributed freely; he has given to the poor; his righteousness endures forever...' Paul quotes this in 2 Corinthians 9 to encourage Christians to give. The point for us to notice is that giving is not generosity but righteousness!

Many Christians today, especially those living in 'Western' cultures, live lives that do not look much different from the lives of their neighbours and work colleagues, except that they attend church. Even when their church is their social circle, they still look like everyone else on social networking sites. They brand themselves like everyone else and get their meaning and motivation from the same influences and people. They want to succeed in the same areas of activity and make money like everyone else. They like to be photographed in the same impressive places and alongside the same status symbols, such as cars, jewellery and clothes.

They desire the same 'must have' lifestyle accessories, eat and drink at the same elegant restaurants and bars. They enjoy the same sorts of entertainments and find the same sorts of things funny. They like to party and goof around just like everyone else. Nobody might ever guess that in their hearts resides a very different set of values!

If Paul could write, 'So, whether you eat or drink, or whatever you do, do all to the glory of God' (1 Corinthians 10:31), then is it not too much to think that something more of the glory of God should be seen in the ways we Christians express ourselves?

Jesus explained the extent to which giving should define our lifestyle generosity with these words. It was and remains radical! 'Love your enemies, do good to those who hate you, bless those who curse you, pray for those who abuse you...and from one who takes away your cloak do not withhold your tunic either. Give to everyone who begs from you, and from one who takes away your goods do not demand them back. And as you wish that others would do to you, do so to them' (Luke 6:27-31).

In the general lifestyle advice in his letter to the Ephesians, Paul explains, 'Let the thief no longer steal, but rather let him labour, doing honest work with his own hands, so that he may have something to share with anyone in need' (Ephesians 4:28). The obligation to provide for people by our work extends beyond providing for our family, our immediate neighbours and the people we know to everyone 'who has need'.

I do not think it is an exaggeration to say that if Jesus' disciples today live as Jesus described, we would not only have a very different attitude towards money and possessions to our neighbours and work colleagues but we would appear to them to be quite mad!

* * *

Questions about tithing usually crop up when Christians discuss giving and so this is a good place to start. Tithing is giving 10% of our income to God, usually to our local church. Some Christians speak of tithes of 5% or some other percentage but this is a contradiction in terms: it is like speaking of three halves of a circle because the Hebrew word translated tithe literally means one tenth.

Some Christians think that tithing is mandatory while others think it is a Jewish practice that Christians do not have to observe. The problem for many churches is that the Christians who believe tithing is non-negotiable usually give 10% but *no more* than 10% of their income, while those who think tithing is legalism usually give less.

Three passages in the Law, the Torah, mention tithing: Leviticus 14 & 27, Numbers 18 and Deuteronomy 14. Read together, they could refer to a single tithe used for three different purposes or to three different tithes. I understand that the religious lawyers in 1st Century Israel understood them as three separate tithes. Additionally, the Law also required sacrifices of animals and crops. Later in Israel's history, a flat rate Temple tax was introduced. It follows that if Christians were to follow the Law's principles, we would give far in excess of 10% and probably somewhere in the region of 30% of our income.

We need to remember that the Law was both a civil and a religious code and in some ways the tithes were the distant ancestor of modern taxes. For example, the Poor Relief Act 1601 was the first modern local tax in the UK, created to give some help to poor people in society, so it fulfilled a similar function to the tithe mentioned in Deuteronomy 14.

I do not think that the tithes prescribed in the Law are binding on Christians because I do not believe that *any* of the Law is binding. As Jesus, the Son of God, on the cross superseded the ancient sacrifices, so they are no longer necessary, so God the Holy Spirit superseded the Law. Christians therefore do not follow the Law but the Holy Spirit. This, however, does **not** mean that we are free to ignore the Law! Paul called it a tutor to bring us to Christ (Galatians 3:24) and one thing we can learn from it is that giving 10% of our income is a very good place to start thinking about giving. I shall return to this point.

Some Christians believe that tithing is mandatory for them because it was done before God gave the Law to Moses. Abraham tithed at least once and Jacob promised to do it if God would look after him. I can see the logic but do not think the situation is quite so clear.

Abraham tithed after he had rescued his nephew Lot and everyone else captured by the armies that invaded Sodom and its allies: the story is told in Genesis 14 and referred to in Hebrews 7. Two references state that Abraham tithed 'everything', but it is not clear to what this refers, while another says that he tithed 'the spoils', but the original Hebrew word does not necessarily refer to what he plundered from the enemy but means, literally, 'the top of the heap'. Genesis explains how Abraham refused to keep anything that he had rescued for the King of Sodom, except what the army had needed to live on, but returned all the liberated goods to the original owners.

Some scholars believe that Abraham tithed all his wealth or all that he had accumulated since arriving in the Promised Land. This interpretation seems to get support from Jacob's commitment to tithe the wealth he accumulates in a foreign country (Genesis 28:20-22). I have heard of churches that follow this principle and each year the members tithe everything they own or their net increase during the previous 12 months.

I think Abraham tithed what he took from the armies that he defeated: the total plunder. He gave Melchizedek a tithe of it all, then returned to the people he has rescued everything that had previously belonged to them (less what his own army had needed to live on) and kept the rest. Abraham's tithe was, I think, his thanksgiving offering to God for Lot's rescue.

I do not know whether Abraham, Jacob (and, by implication, Isaac) tithed routinely or regularly but, if they did, I wonder how they did it. They had no church, temple or tabernacle to support. Did they make repeat visits to Melchizedek? Did they destroy it by sacrifice or give it to the poor? Again, I do not know but I do not need to speculate because I do not think that either the Law or the practice of Abraham and his heirs create an obligation on Christians to tithe. But I do believe they establish a principle. Tithing — giving 10% of our income — is the place to start thinking about structured giving, although it should **not** be the place that we stop thinking about it.

People on persistent low incomes may be justified in giving less than 10%. Unlike in ancient Israel, people's incomes today vary enormously while many living costs are the same for everyone. In the UK, a tithe of £100 from someone on £1,000 a month can be a much greater sacrifice than £500 from someone earning £5,000. Moreover, Jesus criticised the Pharisees for devoting to God money that should have been used to look after their families and Paul wrote that Christians who neglect to take care of their families are worse than unbelievers! These are important things for Christians struggling to make ends meet to keep in mind, to avoid unnecessary guilt about how much they give.

Christians also have a duty to pay taxes and to repay debt. Psalm 37:21 is specific that it is the wicked that do not pay what they owe. (This assumes they are able to repay.) I often wonder what creditors think when they hear Christians say that they cannot pay what they owe because they have to make it a priority to give to their churches.

With those important exceptions in mind, I think Christians today should think about how much they give compared to faithful Jews observing the Law. Just as obedience to the Holy Spirit is superior to obedience to the Torah, I suspect that something may be lacking in our devotion if we are not doing better than they did. But I am confident of one thing! I am sure that God is far more understanding of sincere Christians in difficult circumstances who fail to give 10% than he is of those who could easily give far more than 10% but do not.

Some Christians think that God's promise to the Israelites recorded in Malachi 3, plus Paul's commendation of the Macedonian Christians in 2 Corinthians 8 and Jesus' endorsement of the widow's offering in Mark 12 and Luke 21, assure us of God's provision if we tithe even when we really cannot afford to. These are the three passages.

Bring the full tithe into the storehouse, that there may be food in my house. And thereby put me to the test, says the LORD of hosts, if I will not open the windows of heaven for you and pour down for you a blessing until there is no more need.

For in a severe test of affliction, their abundance of joy and their extreme poverty have overflowed in a wealth of generosity on their part. For they gave according to their means, as I can testify, and beyond their means, of their own accord, begging us earnestly for the favour of taking part in the relief of the saints.

Truly, I tell you, this poor widow has put in more than all of [the rich people]. For they all contributed out of their abundance, but she out of her poverty put in all she had to live on.

We must not over-simplify or jump to conclusions about what these passages teach us. First, the Israelites may have been experiencing hardship due to poor harvests but they were building themselves fine houses and neglecting the Temple restoration. Second, I think that Paul is saying no more about the Macedonian Christians than that were poor, not rich people giving money they would not miss, and that they were prepared to endure additional hardship in order to help others experiencing worse suffering in the famine. Third, there is an obvious and important difference between personal acts of devotion, such as the widow made, and neglecting our families. We may, for example, commend a father who fasted for a period as an act of devotion and in order to increase his giving but not one who refused to feed his children in order to give still more.

Having explained that, I have heard testimonies of people who did make a commitment to give 10% of their inadequate income and found that God made the 90% they kept go further than they would have expected the 100% to have gone. Our God is a faithful God!

Some Christian leaders go a step further and claim that by 'sowing' into their ministry, people can 'reap' an abundant harvest of blessing by getting back from God 30, 50 or 100 times as much as they gave. The parables of the sower told by Jesus, together with Paul's words in 2 Corinthians 9 and Galatians 6, are often cited in support of this. But while sowing and reaping is right, to do it selfishly is self-defeating.

Sowing and reaping is not a means to wealth creation but the way that God created the world to function. The principle is found throughout the Scriptures and applies to much more than money. Proverbs 22 warns that, 'Whoever sows injustice will reap calamity', and Jesus said not to judge or condemn others so that we ourselves will not be judged or condemned. Paul told the Galatians that 'God is not mocked, for whatever one sows, that will he also reap. For the one who sows to his own flesh will from the flesh reap corruption, but the one who sows to the Spirit will from the Spirit reap eternal life.' But having affirmed the generality, it is true that the principle of sowing and reaping includes money. Paul put it like this in 2 Corinthians 9:6-12.

The point is this: whoever sows sparingly will also reap sparingly, and whoever sows bountifully will also reap bountifully. Each one must give as he has decided in his heart, not reluctantly or under compulsion, for God loves a cheerful giver. And God is able to make all grace abound to you, so that having all sufficiency in all things at all times, you may abound in every good work.

As it is written, 'He has distributed freely, he has given to the poor; his righteousness endures forever'. He who supplies seed to the sower and bread for food will supply and multiply your seed for sowing and increase the harvest of your righteousness. You will be enriched in every way to be generous in every way, which through us will produce thanksgiving to God. For the ministry of this service is not only supplying the needs of the saints but is also overflowing in many thanksgivings to God.

It is too simplistic to think that there is some sort of automated payback from God when we give. We should never make the mistake of thinking that our giving in some way puts an obligation on God that is more than his general promise to care for us. But, just as obedience to God's ways changes us, so being obedient in our giving changes us into the people who God can trust with more if he chooses to.

We should not underestimate Paul's assertion that 'God loves a cheerful giver'. It conveys the idea of being both willing and prompt to give but it is as much a reminder to people who organise collections as it is to those who are being encouraged to give. I think it was the incentive for the directions that Paul had given in his earlier letter about how to make the collection he sought (1 Corinthians 16:2).

On the first day of every week, each of you is to put something aside and store it up, as he may prosper, so that there will be no collecting when I come.

I think Paul wanted two things from this. First, he wanted gifts to be proportionate to what people could afford and this was best done on a regular basis: once a week, for the Corinthians, based on how well they had done during the previous week. Today, many Christians may find it more convenient to calculate their gifts once a month or at some other regular intervals. Second, Paul did not want his presence at Corinth to create pressure to give. I do not think he was forbidding collections taken during worship services but I do think he wanted to avoid the sort of incentive to excel that had tempted Ananias and Sapphira. While there must be a degree of transparency and clear accountability in all church finances, there is an obligation on church leaders to organise collections in such a way that people have the personal space and freedom to give *cheerfully*.

By the time you finish this book, I hope that you will understand enough about generosity that your giving will always be cheerful. I hope, too, that if you are responsible for the finances for a church, charity or project that seeks to serve the LORD, you realise that you have no need to put pressure on people to give, so that they end up giving reluctantly from a sense of compulsion.

If there is any financial obligation in the Law that carries over for Christians to take to heart, it is not tithing but caring for the poor. This obligation was not limited to the Israelites' tithes but a much wider generosity woven into their daily lifestyle. Exodus 22:21-27 forbids mistreating strangers, widows and the fatherless. When a loan is necessary, no interest is to be charged and a cloak taken as security had to be returned each night so poor people can stay warm. Among the many wicked things forbidden in Exodus 23:1-11 are being 'partial' to poor people in cases taken to court, which excludes both bias *for and against* them, and perverting the justice due to them.

As well as repeating the prohibitions against oppressing the poor, Leviticus 19:10-15 forbids harvesting a field to its edges or harvesting it twice in order to gather what was missed the first time. It also forbids picking all the grapes in a vineyard or gathering up the grapes that fell of their own accord. All this food was to be left for the poor people to collect for themselves. Employees had to be paid at the end of each day, something the vineyard owner in Jesus' parable remembered but James had to reminded Christians (Matthew 20:8 & James 5:4).

Foreigners living in ancient Israel were not to be treated as second-class citizens but in the same way as brother Israelites. They deserved the same standard of justice and fairness and, by implication, could expect to receive the same quality of generosity as poor and vulnerable Israelites. Leviticus 19:33-34 is explicit! 'When a stranger sojourns with you in your land, you shall not do him wrong. You shall treat the stranger who sojourns with you as the native among you, and you shall love him as yourself, for you were strangers in the land of Egypt: I am the LORD your God.'

The rest of the Hebrew Scriptures, the 'Law and the Prophets', emphasise concern for the poor as a key responsibility necessary to please God. Psalms and Proverbs state repeatedly that God has a special concern for the poor and that people who fail to help them are wicked. The prophets repeatedly criticised the Israelites for neglecting the poor. Neglect of the poor brought God's judgement on many nations, including Babylon as well as both Israel and Judah. In the New Testament, it was concern for the poor that Paul and the church leaders in Jerusalem agreed on as a necessary obligation.

Paul's words quoted at the start of this chapter are similar to what Samuel said when he stood down as Israel's last judge, to make way for Saul to be its first king. He asked the people to confirm that he had not used his position to defraud or oppress anyone nor taken bribes. The people responded, 'You have not defrauded us or oppressed us or taken anything from any man's hand' (1 Samuel 12:1-5). This was important to Samuel because he had appointed his sons as judges but they 'took bribes and perverted justice' (1 Samuel 8:1-3).

Many of the Pharisees who opposed Jesus behaved badly and I think it was because Paul had been a Pharisee that he wanted to distinguish his own ministry from them. He also wanted to differentiate himself from the many teachers who took advantage of their status in churches to exploit God's people for personal gain. In his letter to the church at Corinth, he explains how Christian ministry should be funded in the same way as the ministry at the Temple in Jerusalem, by donations from the worshippers. He explains this to affirm his right to their financial support but — crucially! — he did so **not** to claim the right but to waive it. We should consider carefully the reasons he gave in 1 Corinthians 19:13-19.

> *Do you not know that those who are employed in the temple service get their food from the temple, and those who serve at the altar share in the sacrificial offerings? In the same way, the Lord commanded that those who proclaim the gospel should get their living by the gospel. But I have made no use of any of these rights, nor am I writing these things to secure any such provision. For I would rather die than have anyone deprive me of my ground for boasting. For if I preach the gospel, that gives me no ground for boasting. For necessity is laid upon me. Woe to me if I do not preach the gospel! For if I do this of my own will, I have a reward, but if not of my own will, I am still entrusted with a stewardship. What then is my reward? That in my preaching I may present the gospel free of charge, so as not to make full use of my right in the gospel. For though I am free from all, I have made myself a servant to all, that I might win more of them.*

I would summarise Paul's attitude like this. He believed that he had no choice but to preach the Gospel as God had called him to do. It therefore gave him no cause to boast! But, in order to please the LORD and to be worthy of a reward in heaven, he ought to do something above and beyond what God had called him to do. He wanted to do something good that was not required of him. He therefore preached *without charge*.

All churches have a duty to support their ministers. I would even go a little further and say that churches should support their ministers to approximately the same standard of living that most of the church members enjoy. There will be exceptions to this but, in my view, the decision to serve on a unfairly low income should be the minister's and not the congregation's choice. Unfortunately, during the 40 years I have been a Christian, I have come across examples of churches that presume upon their ministers' sense of vocation and obligation to remain on a low income or in poor living conditions. Some churches let their ministers' homes become run down, only authorising repair work and redecoration when a minister leaves and the church has to attract a new minister.

I suspect that Paul desired to minister without being a burden on the people he taught for another reason also. In Romans 15:20-21, he explains that, 'I make it my ambition to preach the gospel, not where Christ has already been named...' I am sure that he was aware of the impression it would create if he arrived in a place that had never heard of Jesus, preach the Gospel, and then, as soon as people believed his message, ask them for money. I think that churches and evangelists today should be just as careful when they 'take offerings'.

The impression I have from reading passages such as Acts 20:34, 1 Corinthians 4:12, Philippians 4:10-19, 1 Thessalonians 2:9 & 4:11 and 2 Thessalonians 3:8 is that although some churches and individual Christians donated to his ministry, most of the time Paul worked to earn the money he needed. When he could, I expect that he made tents, as Acts 18:2-3 suggests. But this was his choice! A choice he made willingly in the service of Jesus who said that, contrary to what most people think, it is more blessed to give than to receive.

I often hear ministers say that they 'hate' talking about money and, when they do, sounding terribly apologetic. I understand why they talk like this but I fear that it does more harm than good because the use and abuse of money is an important subject that needs to be taught and discussed by Christians. What is a mistake, I think, is to talk about it when trying to raise funds because then it comes across as self-serving. In the same way as a spirit of utility is uncouth when coming to God, because God should be sought for his own sake and not for what we can hope to get from him, even in a worthy cause, so to teach about money with an ulterior motive is manipulative. Preachers and teachers should educate and encourage, not manipulate!

In the same way as some churches will not act on what they believe is God's call without the funding already assured, a financial problem for an on-going project is more likely to be perceived as God prompting a change of direction rather than as an incentive to pray for resources. In fact, I have the impression that some Christians think it unsustainable to 'pray in' finances each year, although I have never heard any say so explicitly. Of course, God can use financial issues to signal his disapproval but we should not jump to conclusions. We must be more discerning than to risk 'cutting down a rose tree on the very day it was blossoming', to use the analogy offered 100 years ago by the director of a very successful mission under threat of closure for lack of funds. It was at about this time that Christians in Europe and America were turning from giving to fundraising.

We see in the Bible how God provides for his people in a variety of ways. The most common is for every Christian to work. Paul said that, 'If a man will not work, he shall not eat' (2 Timothy 3:10). He was assuming that the worker was able to work and that paid work was available, as we can infer from the New Testament teaching to look after poor and vulnerable people.

God sometimes provides for us by amazing 'coincidences'. I have put coincidences in quotation marks because I think that God is sovereign and there are no truly random accidents. After using Simon Peter's boat as a makeshift pulpit, Jesus told him to go into the lake and let down his nets (Luke 5:3-11). Having worked all night without success, Peter thought this hopeless but in fact caught so many fish he had to call another boat to help. I expect some people saw this as a fluke but something similar happened when Jesus met his disciples after his resurrection (John 21:5-11).

On another occasion, in order to pay the Temple Tax, Jesus instructed Peter to catch a single fish and, when he did so, he found a coin in the fish's mouth (Matthew 17:27). No doubt, some saw this as amazing good luck!

On at least two occasions, Jesus multiplied a few loaves and fishes to feed large crowds. I know some people think that the offer of loaves and fishes inspired others to share the food they had with them but I do not think this is what happened. They were miracles, as the Gospels describe. Nevertheless, I doubt that many of the people in the crowd were aware of just what had actually happened but assumed the obvious explanation.

When God works miracles for us, they are often discreet and easily taken for granted. As the Israelites trekked through the wilderness for 40 years, their clothes and shoes did not wear out and their feet did not get sore. Something else the Israelites soon began to take for granted was the provision of food and water. They usually found water in quite natural ways but when necessary it flowed from seemingly barren rock. When the people pleaded for food, a huge flock of birds fell out of the sky near their camp! These events are described in Exodus 17, Deuteronomy 8 (see also Nehemiah 9:21) and Numbers 11 & 20 and we must not overlook or underestimate just how *ungrateful* the people were for God's goodness. We must be better than they were!

Most remarkable of all was the way that God provided for the Israelites was the manna, that is described in Exodus 16. Six out of seven days each week, the Israelites went out early in the morning to collect fresh manna. If they kept any of it until the next day, it turned rotten. But the seventh day, the Sabbath, was different. This was a mandatory day of rest. The manna collected the previous day did not rot overnight and there was no fresh manna to be found in the morning. There can be no natural explanation for this!

When Elijah was faithful in proclaiming a drought throughout Israel, God directed him first to an isolated brook where ravens dropped bread they had scavenged for him and, later, to lodge with a widow whose flour and oil did not run out. When the drought was past, but the land had not had time to recover, the Lord sent to Elijah an angel with a meal.

The ability to work, however, remains the most common way for God's people to provide for their needs and to provide for others who need their help. God was the first worker, creating the heavens and the earth. He worked until he had finished and then he instituted the Sabbath as a day of necessary rest.

There are many passages in the Bible about the need for people to work but in the creation we understand that it was required even in paradise. While we may not know all that Adam and Eve had to do, because there was no need to water or weed, human effort and skill were important. They exercised their discretion, such as when they named all the animals, and made a valuable contribution to God's finished creation.

Sin may have brought weariness and frustration to the human experience of work but, essentially, work is not something we do because we have to but because of what we are. It is not something we should do to take from creation but what we do to preserve and develop creation. We therefore make one of the greatest blunders of our lives when we choose a career rather than discover our calling.

King Solomon discovered something fascinating about work that he documented in his great thesis on the meaning of life, which is in the Bible and called Ecclesiastes. Solomon was arguably the wealthiest person who ever lived. There may be people today with greater wealth stored as credit data in computer systems but none who could convert it into the volume of material wealth that Solomon owned. In 1 Kings 10, we read that he drank only from gold cups and at his official residence everything was made of gold. There was so much gold in the Kingdom that 'silver was not considered as anything' and in Jerusalem it was as common as stones.

Solomon's unrestrained materialism illustrates the weaker side of his character. The way he continued to accumulate wealth, particularly through all the trading expeditions he sponsored, betrayed his avarice. Whether it was luxury itself or his ruinous choice of wives and the foreign gods he tolerated that corrupted him, the Bible focuses more on his excesses than on his wisdom. Although he stands an example of how wealth can create greater temptations than poverty, for all this, Solomon was one of the wisest people who ever lived. His great wealth enabled him to do anything he wanted and he decided to study pleasure! He records what happened in Ecclesiastes 2:1-11.

I said in my heart, 'Come now, I will test you with pleasure; enjoy yourself.' But behold, this also was vanity. I said of laughter, 'It is mad,' and of pleasure, 'What use is it?' I searched with my heart how to cheer my body with wine — my heart still guiding me with wisdom — and how to lay hold on folly, till I might see what was good for the children of man to do under heaven during the few days of their life. I made great works. I built

houses and planted vineyards for myself. I made myself gardens and parks,
and planted in them all kinds of fruit trees. I made myself pools from which
to water the forest of growing trees. I bought male and female slaves, and
had slaves who were born in my house. I had also great possessions of
herds and flocks, more than any who had been before me in Jerusalem. I
also gathered for myself silver and gold and the treasure of kings and
provinces. I got singers, both men and women, and many concubines, the
delight of the children of man. So I became great and surpassed all who
were before me in Jerusalem. Also my wisdom remained with me. And
whatever my eyes desired I did not keep from them. I kept my heart from no
pleasure, for my heart found pleasure in all my toil, and this was my
reward for all my toil. Then I considered all that my hands had done and
the toil I had expended in doing it, and behold, all was vanity and a striving
after wind, and there was nothing to be gained under the sun.

Solomon's conclusion from all his activity was that, 'All was vanity and a striving after wind...' But just before he recorded this conclusion, he noted that 'My heart found pleasure in all my toil; and this was my reward from all my toil'. The pleasure that King Solomon got from his work was the only pleasure he got from his pursuit of pleasure.

Solomon's work was his pleasure because work is a fundamental part of what it is to be fully human. God did not create us to live idly but to contribute our industry and art to his creation. Many people are limited in the work they do, and not everyone is paid, but everyone has the capacity to contribute positively and constructively to God's creation.

In Ephesians 4:28, Paul explained one aspect of this contribution that we often overlook, when he wrote that reformed thieves should work in order to have something to share with people in need. This is more than an exhortation limited to criminals and others who once accumulated wealth unscrupulously but a guiding principle for all Christians. The obligation to provide for others by our work extends beyond providing for our families, our immediate neighbours and the people we know. It embraces everyone 'who has need'.

When we grasp this, it takes us far beyond structured giving. Issues about tithing evaporate as unimportant and Christians, especially those living in consumer societies, are easily identified when they really believed that it is more blessed to give than to receive.

Jesus explained the extent to which giving should define our lifestyles with these words. 'Love your enemies, do good to those who hate you, bless those who curse you, pray for those who abuse you...and from one who takes away your cloak do not withhold your tunic either. Give to everyone who begs from you, and from one who takes away your goods do not demand them back. And as you wish that others would do to you, do so to them' (Luke 6:27-31). Paul took this literally. 'Contribute to the needs of the saints and seek to show hospitality', he wrote towards the end of Romans 12. 'Bless those who persecute you; bless and do not curse them... Repay no one evil for evil... If possible, so far as it depends on you, live peaceably with all.' His next statement is unequivocal. 'Beloved, never avenge yourselves, but leave it to the wrath of God, for it is written, "Vengeance is mine, I will repay, says the Lord".'

But are their limits to such straightforward counsel? As we walk along a city street, should we give to any homeless or destitute person who asks us for money, even if we think they are likely to do themselves harm by using it to buy alcohol or drugs? If someone asks to borrow from us, either our money or our possessions, should we automatically comply even if they have a reputation for dishonesty? I think the clue is implicit in what Jesus said in his Sermon on the Mount. This is Matthew 5:38-48.

You have heard that it was said, 'An eye for an eye and a tooth for a tooth.' But I say to you, Do not resist the one who is evil. But if anyone slaps you on the right cheek, turn to him the other also. And if anyone would sue you and take your tunic, let him have your cloak as well. And if anyone forces you to go one mile, go with him two miles. Give to the one who begs from you, and do not refuse the one who would borrow from you.

You have heard that it was said, 'You shall love your neighbour and hate your enemy.' But I say to you, Love your enemies and pray for those who persecute you, so that you may be sons of your Father who is in heaven... For if you love those who love you, what reward do you have? Do not even the tax collectors do the same? And if you greet only your brothers, what more are you doing than others? Do not even the Gentiles do the same? You therefore must be perfect, as your heavenly Father is perfect.

'Do not resist an evil person'! The 'evil' that Jesus referred to was not illegality but taking advantage of people from positions of political or social superiority. It does not mean that Christian police officers should overlook crime or that Christian judges should pardon it.

The slap on the cheek was not the start of a brawl but an insulting backhanded slap: most people are right-handed and so a slap to someone's *right* cheek (Jesus was specific about this) must be done with the back of the hand. Being taken to court for both cloak and tunic represents harsh action by creditors: it was forbidden in Jewish Law but allowed under Roman law. Going the extra mile illustrates oppressive demands by State officials: Roman soldiers in occupied countries could require citizens to carry their baggage and equipment for one mile.

Today, we might have to endure embarrassing breaches of confidence by neighbours, malicious rumours started by work colleagues and gross misrepresentation by business rivals. Disaffected members of our family or people we thought of as friends might use gossip and lies to discredit us. Someone who knows that we cannot afford to defend a claim might threaten us with expensive legal action just to get their own way. Businesses and government departments may deny liability for errors and injustices, hoping we cannot afford the expense of court action to get the compensation we need. Careless or indifferent government officials may put us to a lot of cost and inconvenience dealing with their needless impositions.

Jesus described peaceful responses to the situations he outlined but in ways that asserted the victims' freedom from oppression. Turning the other cheek makes a second backhanded slap difficult, making the oppressor look clumsy and incompetent. For a person in debt to be stripped of both tunic and cloak would publicly expose the creditor as punitive. A Roman solider could be disciplined for letting a civilian carry his baggage for two miles. Jesus wanted his followers to respond to all injustices with similar creativity and pragmatism. He did not want them to react instinctively, to 'fight fire with fire', even when confident of being in the right. We who seek to live as citizens of the Kingdom of God today need to act with this sort of inspired freedom.

'Love your enemies'! As in dealing with evil people, Jesus is encouraging righteous pragmatism. At a basic level, we should not believe everything enemies say or that we hear about them. We should not be so quick as to assume they are in need if they have a track record of deception.

We are not to give to just anyone we see begging but we do need to overcome any social prejudice we may feel about homeless and poor people: this is especially important if they are from another country or practice a different religion. We may have to forgive and overlook any wrong they may have done to us in the past. We will need to be clear on the help they think they need and what they actually need and be careful not to give them the means to do harm, either to themselves or to others. But when a situation is clear, and a need confirmed, positive and supportive action is required.

On another occasion, Jesus referred to a rich man and a beggar to illustrate how easy it is to be complacent about loving our neighbours as ourselves.

There was a rich man who was clothed in purple and fine linen and who feasted sumptuously every day. And at his gate was laid a poor man named Lazarus, covered with sores, who desired to be fed with what fell from the rich man's table. Moreover, even the dogs came and licked his sores. The poor man died and was carried by the angels to Abraham's side. The rich man also died and was buried, and in Hades, being in torment, he lifted up his eyes and saw Abraham far off and Lazarus at his side. And he called out, 'Father Abraham, have mercy on me, and send Lazarus to dip the end of his finger in water and cool my tongue, for I am in anguish in this flame.'

The rich man did not abuse poor, sick Lazarus. He may well have given Lazarus leftover food, which is why Lazarus stayed at the gates to the estate. I would not be surprised to learn that Lazarus got unwanted clothing and other modest help from the rich man and his servants. But the rich man's offence was that he failed to love Lazarus *as himself*. The two men may have been at opposite ends of the social spectrum but they were neighbours.

Jesus illustrated what it means to love our enemies in the story known as the Parable of the Good Samaritan. In Luke 10:30-35, we read how a Jew is mugged and left on the road between Jerusalem and Jericho. Two fellow Jews, a priest and a Levite (a temple official), walked past him, unwilling to help. A Samaritan then approaches.

The Jews and Samaritans had been natural enemies for centuries: although they often lived as neighbours, they despised and mistrusted each other. Of the three men who saw the injured Israelite lying in the road, the Samaritan would have seemed to Jesus' audience as the one most likely to finish what the robbers had started, taking anything they had missed and even striking a fatal blow! Yet, this is the man who stopped to help and then went out of his way to give the injured man the best possible chance of making a full recovery.

I can picture the man lying a few metres from the road, perhaps among or near some rocks. The priest and the Levite may have walked past because they feared the man might be a decoy or left as bait, in the hope that someone would stop to help and become the robbers' next victim when they leapt from their hiding places. People today share that fear. Did the Samaritan share it? I expect so. But he stopped anyway!

If their religion meant anything to them at all, the priest and the Levite should have trusted God, stopped and helped. Clearly, they did not trust God enough to look after them while loving their neighbour. The Samaritan not only stopped long enough to tend to the man's wounds but also took him to the safety of an inn. And he went further! He not only paid for his immediate care but also promised to pay for any further treatment the man needed. In effect, the Samaritan wrote a 'blank cheque' and, in doing so, trusted both the injured Israelite and the innkeeper not to take advantage of his generosity!

The Jew and the Samaritan may have felt like each other's enemies but their proximity to each other made them neighbours and their story illustrates what it means to love our enemies and to give or lend to those in need. But Jesus did not stop there! Preserved for us in John 13:34-35, he explained how anyone in the world, in every age, would be able to identify his disciples.

*A new commandment I give to you, that you love one another: just as I have loved you, you also are to love one another. By this all people will know that you are my disciples, **if you have love for one another.***

The implication is clear! Claims of religious allegiance, spiritual devotion and even right theology are inadequate to distinguish true Christians from the rest of society. Only Christians' love for each another will do that! But the lack of love among the Christians at Corinth was very public!

Paul criticised the way they met together to remember Jesus in what he called The Lord's Supper but what we now call by a variety of other names, including Breaking Bread, Holy Communion, Eucharist and Mass. It seems that those who arrived first ate and drank all they wanted, partying well and leaving nothing for those who arrived later. This reflected the social divide: the richer Christians arriving first but those who had to work longer hours, like servants and slaves, arriving later. As a result, 'one goes hungry, another gets drunk'! Paul stated bluntly that such behaviour despised the church and humiliated those who had nothing (1 Corinthians 11:17-34).

Paul also criticised the way the Christian businessmen took each other to court. This was not to resolve genuine disputes in areas of legitimate difference of opinion but to expose each other's cheating! The advice he gave was probably hard to swallow. 'Why not rather suffer wrong?' he wrote, 'Why not rather be defrauded?' (1 Corinthians 6:1-11).

Why? The court cases exposed to the entire city how dishonest Christians could be. It must have completely undermined their witness! In recommending that someone within the church resolve the disputes, Paul was not concerned simply with the need for discretion but he wanted them to deal with the dishonesty.

In a previous passage in the letter, Paul had explained that the Christians were not to associate with people who called themselves Christian but did not live the sort of life that Jesus described for his disciples. He later reminded them, 'Do you not know that the unrighteous will not inherit the kingdom of God? Do not be deceived: neither the sexually immoral, nor idolaters, nor adulterers, nor men who practice homosexuality, nor thieves, nor the greedy [literally, covetous], nor drunkards, nor revilers, nor swindlers will inherit the kingdom of God.' See 1 Corinthians 5:9-13 and 1 Corinthians 6:9-10.

Rather than try to get compensation in the courts, it was better for the Christians to suffer the loss and to disassociate themselves from Christians who behaved so very badly. If more churches acted on Paul's advice today, their congregations may shrink but I am sure their witness would flourish!

Jesus of Nazareth wanted people to love God with their whole selves and to love their neighbours as themselves. He wanted them to love their enemies and their persecutors. And love for one another was the hallmark of his disciples. Paul summarised brilliantly the nature of this love in his famous passage we now know as 1 Corinthians 13, often read at weddings.

After explaining that even if he had the ability to speak in many languages, even the languages of angels, and if he had prophetic powers that enabled him to understand all mysteries and all knowledge, and if he had sufficient faith to order mountains to move and to offer himself for martyrdom, it would not amount to much if he did not also have love. Without love, it would all be just so much noise, amounting to nothing! Then he explained what love is, not with a dictionary definition but by example.

> *Love is patient and kind; love does not envy or boast; it is not arrogant or rude. It does not insist on its own way; it is not irritable or resentful; it does not rejoice at wrongdoing, but rejoices with the truth. Love bears all things, believes all things, hopes all things, endures all things. Love never ends.*

John wrote a lot about love. He defined God's essential character as 'God is love' (1 John 4:8 & 16) and when he defined love itself he did not use adjectives but example. 'By this we know love' he wrote, 'that [Jesus] laid down his life for us'. He then appends this challenge, 'And we ought to lay down our lives for the brothers' (1 John 3:16).

With this in mind, I offer a criteria for thinking and praying about giving, based on the commandment to love our neighbours as ourselves. *How does your spending on **conveniences** and **pleasures** compare with your **giving**?* You may be making purchases that seem reasonable to you, and are modest in comparison to the people around you, but when the amount you spend on these *exceeds* what you give to help others, it is an indication of the extent to which you love your neighbours as yourself.

5: One who is faithful in a very little is also faithful in much

One who is faithful in a very little is also faithful in much, and one who is dishonest in a very little is also dishonest in much. If then you have not been faithful in the unrighteous wealth, who will entrust to you the true riches? And if you have not been faithful in that which is another's, who will give you that which is your own? No servant can serve two masters, for either he will hate the one and love the other, or he will be devoted to the one and despise the other. You cannot serve God and money.
Luke 16:10-13

WHEN JESUS REFERRED to 'very little', he meant 'unrighteous mammon'. He was not referring to a small amount of money but to money itself. Older translations use the phrase, 'that which is least', which I think better expresses the relative unimportance of money. The power of money in the world may not seem unimportant to us, and a lot of people may believe it to be very important, but Jesus saw it for what it is.

Some modern Bibles, including the English Standard Version that I quote in this book, refer to unrighteous mammon as 'unrighteous wealth' or 'wicked riches' but, as we have seen already, not all wealth is unrighteous. Mammon, however, is *always* unrighteous because of its corrupting power over people.

The 'much' that Jesus mentioned is 'true riches', or spiritual wealth. In the above passage, Jesus was not saying that integrity in the little things matters. That is important but Jesus was making another point. He was explaining that Christians who cannot handle faithfully the material wealth entrusted to them by God for this life, cannot be trusted with true spiritual riches for this life or for the life to follow.

The material wealth we enjoy now is not really ours to keep: it really belongs to 'another'. It really belongs to God. We have what we have by the grace of God and we handle it as God's stewards. And how we handle it has eternal consequences.

While it is usually quite easy to persuade Christians of the truth of this, it is very much harder to make the implications clear. Like the rich young ruler who could not transfer his trust from his inherited wealth to God alone, many Christians think their security and significance depends on their property, goods and savings. Even when they believe it is God's blessing, they go to great lengths to accumulate and protect money. They do this even though history is full of examples of how isolated acts of foolishness and events happening far away can wither the greatest fortunes.

In a number of his parables, Jesus talked about the responsibility of servants while their masters are away. In a few of them, masters going abroad give resources to their servants and, on their return, reward those servants with varying degrees of responsibility, based on what they did during their absence. The parables therefore speak to our responsibility as Christians here and now using the resources that God entrusts to us and the reward that awaits us in the future, based on how we handled those resources.

Death is not the end of this life and the start of something new but a development that stretches forward from this life: how we live now will determine how we will live then. Paul talked about this explicitly in two of his letters, explaining that, 'We must all appear before the judgment seat of Christ, so that each one may receive what is due for what he has done in the body...' (2 Corinthians 5:10).

The choice that Jesus was putting to his disciples was between living like most people in society, for our own advantage, and living the sort of life he describes in the Sermon on the Mount and the rest of his teaching: a life appropriate for people who are citizens of the Kingdom of God.

We should take a moment to remind ourselves that the Kingdom of God is a place of spiritual values. 'The kingdom of God is not a matter of eating and drinking', Paul wrote in Romans 14:17, 'but of righteousness and peace and joy in the Holy Spirit'. The fundamental commandments for Kingdom living are utter allegiance to God and loving our neighbours as ourselves. We do not crave autonomy or exalt ourselves, trying to be like God as Lucifer wanted to be like him, but follow Jesus' example of dependence and sacrifice. In the Kingdom, the meek inherit the earth and the humble are exalted; the greatest are those who serve most. It is a place very different from the ways of human society and therefore it is not just unnecessary for Christians to use money like everyone else but ultimately self-defeating.

I have an embarrassing theory. I think that society's general rejection of the message about Jesus and the failure of Christians to have much impact on social values and morality is a result of widespread failure among Christians to handle material wealth properly. Having, for the most part, bought into capitalism and the primacy of money, and living lifestyles largely indistinguishable from everyone else in a consumer society, we Christians have demonstrated our unwillingness and inability to handle money God's way, in line with the principles of the Kingdom that Jesus taught.

If that were to change, so that more Christians and churches could be trusted with spiritual riches, we might see revival more often. First and foremost, we would see more practical love among Christians for each other and for their neighbours. We would see and hear the Gospel, the Good News about Jesus, proclaimed with greater clarity and conviction, so that fewer people could ignore it. We would see Jesus' teaching having a wider impact on society, as the moral imperatives that flow from the Gospel become irresistible to the people who believe and trust in God.

I expect we would see more use of the gifts of the Holy Spirit identified by Paul in Romans 12 and 1 Corinthians 12-14. These include wisdom, knowledge, faith, generosity, service, teaching, healing, miracles, prophecy, spiritual perception, tongues and the interpretation of tongues. 'All these are empowered by one and the same Spirit, who *apportions to each one individually* as he wills.'

* * *

In my experience, a lot of 'Christian' teaching about giving and stewardship stops short at setting out principles and standards for making the most of God's material blessings. I have found a lot of this teaching helpful and know that it helps a lot of people, especially those in debt or struggling to make ends meet. But even when financial principles are drawn from Scripture, they often fail to touch the deepest recesses of our hearts and our minds, so that we continue to function in society in much the same way as everyone else. We may not be so extravagant and we may be a little more compassionate and generous but we still see money as the means — the God-given means — to live well.

Another thing that troubles me slightly about some personal finance teaching by Christians is that it leaves people thinking more about money than about God. I understand why that might be inevitable in the short term. It is like a person with a weight problem who needs to diet. For a while, they have to examine food labels and diligently count the calories they consume. Similarly, a person in debt or struggling to make ends meet will, for a while, need to spend quite a lot of time planning their spending and monitoring their bank account. But as a food diet should help establish good eating habits and healthy lifestyle, so that the person needs to think less and less about food, so another person getting their financial situation sorted out should practice self-discipline and learn contentment and move towards the point where money does not take too much of their attention.

I know, of course, that very many people diet for a time, to meet some short or medium term goal, and then return to their unhealthy eating habits. They usually end up having to repeat the process later. I pray that this book will be the only incentive you need to leave you thinking more about God than money into the future.

There is nothing at all wrong with financial stability and material comforts: they **are** God's blessing! But if they are all it takes to satisfy Christians, then it is all just treasure on earth. Paul warned of this situation in 2 Timothy 3.

In the last days there will come times of difficulty. For people will be lovers of self, lovers of money, proud, arrogant, abusive, disobedient to their parents, ungrateful, unholy, heartless, unappeasable, slanderous, without self-control, brutal, not loving good, treacherous, reckless, swollen with conceit, lovers of pleasure rather than lovers of God, having the appearance of godliness, but denying its power...

A form of religion! A type of Christianity! But no power in it! Learned, intellectually viable, financially astute, carefully aspiring to good stewardship, moral and respectable, but content with a reputation built upon the unremarkable and unable to proclaim the Gospel with a power to convict people and empower them to live in the ways of the Kingdom of God. And little or no power to prophesy and heal. (Does this description seem familiar to you?)

I previously mentioned two parables where Jesus explained that treasure in heaven is responsibility in the Kingdom of God. They are recorded in Matthew 25:14-30 and Luke 19:12-28 and in both of them men going abroad gave resources to their servants. In one of the parables, three servants were entrusted with different amounts, which I think refers to the varying spiritual gifts given to us individually; in the other, ten servants each received one mina (or pound), which I think refers to the same Gospel message or the same Holy Spirit we all have. On their return, the men rewarded their servants with varying degrees of responsibility, based on what they had done with the resources.

In the parable in Matthew, the servant given five talents makes five more, the one given three makes three more but the servant given just one talent buries it in the ground for fear of displeasing his master. The master had distributed the talents according to each servant's ability. The two who returned double did equally well but the servant who returned only the one was rebuked. All he had needed to do to be as successful as the other servants was to return *just one more.*

Jesus told the parable that Luke records as he approached Jerusalem for the last time because his disciples still thought his mission would culminate there with the overthrow of Roman rule. This is why, in this version, the master is going away to a foreign country to receive a kingdom.

Of the ten servants each given a mina, we hear only how well three of them did. One returned ten times as much and another returned five times but one returned only the one mina that he had been given. Like the servant in the other parable, he had hidden his investment, gave the same excuse and was rebuked.

In both parables, the masters turned the excuses back on their useless servants. 'I will condemn you with your own words, you wicked servant! You knew that I was a severe man, taking what I did not deposit and reaping what I did not sow? Why then did you not put my money in the bank, and at my coming I might have collected it with interest?' Neither man was agreeing with his servants' assessment but only pointing out that if the servants had really believed what they said, they should at least have acted consistently with their belief. If they had really thought their masters to be 'severe' men, they should have deposited their investment with bankers, so their masters could have at least received interest on the money.

To invest the money like this would have been far from ideal. Interest, called usury across the ancient world and forbidden in the Jewish Law, was widely considered immoral even where it was legal. Only unscrupulous men who hoped to reap what they had not sown took interest. But if the servants had really believed their own excuses, the interest would have been better than nothing!

I want to speculate on these two parables and ask, *When the useless servants hid their investments, what did they do with their time?* I realise that I may be pushing the application a little too far but I hope you will see what I am getting at. Were they idle? Did they waste their time with hobbies and entertainment? Did they forget whose servants they were and hire themselves out to other masters?

As these parables are about how Jesus' disciples should behave during his absence, we can get a clue to how the useless servants behaved by looking at the other parables on the same subject. In Matthew 24:45-51, we read of other servants left in charge of their master's property. In this case, the 'wise servant' did his duty and looked after the servants under him, giving 'their food at the proper time'. But, the 'wicked servant said to himself, "My master is delayed", and begins to beat his fellow servants and eats and drinks with drunkards'.

It seems reasonable to me to conclude that the useless servants who hid their investments either abused their positions of responsibility or mixed with bad company. Or both. They no doubt continued to live on their masters' estates and fed and clothed themselves at their masters' expense but they did not do more than necessary to look after their masters' affairs.

What about us? If we are not trading with the investment that God has given us while we await Jesus' return, is it because we have forgotten whose servants we are? Do we mix with bad company? Perhaps not getting drunk but drinking in enough that we can see no harm in adopting society's values and ways, and so compromise our allegiance to God!

Are we content living like everyone else, accumulating possessions and storing up treasurers on earth, enjoying what everyone else enjoys? Are we about our divine master's business no more than is necessary?

In two letters, Romans 14:10-12 and 2 Corinthians 5:10, Paul refers to the judgment seat of Christ, the place where Christians will receive the reward for what they have done in this life. In the former, Paul mentions it to dissuade his readers from being judgemental; in the latter, to persuade us to preserve in living in the light of spiritual values.

The original Greek words used by Paul describe not just appearing at the judgement seat, like a person may appear in court, but in being *made manifest* there. Our true selves will be known! Nothing superficial about us will delude the judge!

Some Christians think this involves a virtual re-run of our entire lives on earth, as if on video. I do not think this will necessarily happen but it is the occasion when the true nature of our personalities will be exposed and how we have behaved in this life will be seen as either good or evil.

The quotation at the start of this chapter was spoken on a day in Jesus' ministry when he confronted some Pharisees about their love of money. It is recorded in Luke 14:1-17:10. The origin of the Pharisees is not entirely clear but they seem to have formed as a distinct Jewish sect about 400 years earlier, during or soon after a revolt against the banning of religious ritual by their foreign rulers. They were especially devoted to keeping the Torah, the Law, and by the time Jesus walked in Israel, the Pharisees were an elite, a major part of the 'establishment'.

It is important to remember that not all of the Pharisees that Jesus met were corrupt. Some were sincerely devout men who Jesus helped understand the truth. But I think it is fair to say that many of them were trying so hard to please God that they got lost in the detail of the Law. By reflecting on what Jesus told them, we hold up a mirror to our own lives.

The day of the confrontation was a Sabbath, a day of rest. The difficulties started with an invitation to a meal at the home of a ruling Pharisee. There was a sick man present and everyone watched to see if Jesus would heal him. The invitation was a set up. The Pharisee would not normally have invited the man but did so to provoke Jesus.

I am sure that Jesus knew it was a trap. He dealt with the flawed theology head on by asserting the overriding responsibility to show compassion. 'Which of you having a son or an ox that has fallen into a well on a Sabbath day, will not immediately pull him out?' he asked, referring to the common practice. He then healed the man and sent him away.

Jesus then criticised the other guests for their pride in wanting to sit in the places of honour rather than show the humility that commends God's people. 'Then you will be honoured in the presence of all who sit at table with you. For everyone who exalts himself will be humbled, and he who humbles himself will be exalted'. He also criticised his host for only inviting people who could return the hospitality rather than people who needed help and would appreciate the food and fellowship much more: the poor, sick and disabled. The Pharisee should not have invited just one sick man to the banquet but many. 'You will be blessed', he explained, 'because they cannot repay you.' Referring to treasure in heaven, he then added, 'For you will be repaid at the resurrection of the just'.

Jesus then told the Parable of the Great Banquet, to explain how the privileged that were complacent about the ways of the Kingdom of God would be excluded from it but the poor, sick and disabled would be welcome.

The Pharisees' wealth should have been their opportunity to serve people less well off than themselves. This is why Luke states explicitly that they were lovers of money. Notwithstanding their claim to be devoted to the Law, these Pharisees understood neither it nor the God who had given it to Moses. Instead, they sought to promote themselves in public and assert their theological superiority at the expense of others. In this, they followed in the footsteps of Lucifer, who worked for his own self-aggrandisement. This is why, on another occasion Jesus told them, 'You are of your father the devil, and your will is to do your father's desires...' (John 8:44).

By contrast, we should reflect on Jesus' own attitude, as described by Paul in Philippians 2:3-11. Jesus did not consider it important to cling to the privileges of Godhead but took a downward course to redeem people who could not help themselves.

Do nothing from rivalry or conceit, but in humility count others more significant than yourselves. Let each of you look not only to his own interests, but also to the interests of others. Have this mind among yourselves, which is yours in Christ Jesus, who, though he was in the form of God, did not count equality with God a thing to be grasped, but made himself nothing, taking the form of a servant, being born in the likeness of men. And being found in human form, he humbled himself by becoming obedient to the point of death, even death on a cross. Therefore God has highly exalted him and bestowed on him the name that is above every name, so that at the name of Jesus every knee should bow, in heaven and on earth and under the earth, and every tongue confess that Jesus Christ is Lord, to the glory of God the Father.

Jesus did not stop being God but gave up his *status* and *privileges* as God. By behaving this way, he aspired to the very opposite ambition that had motivated Lucifer, Adam and Eve and Nebuchadnezzar. In response, the Father 'highly exalted him' — doing the very thing for Jesus that he had refused to do for himself.

Jesus left the banquet. He criticised the Pharisees' elitism and explained that his own disciples needed to put him and his cause ahead of their own families and to each take up their own cross. We know from what he said on other occasions, and from the letters preserved for us in the New Testament, that Jesus was not suggesting that Christians neglect their families but setting priorities. As he put it in the Sermon on the Mount, 'Seek *first* the Kingdom of God and his righteousness'. That priority comes before everything else, although Christians who neglect to provide for their families are not living righteously.

Jesus illustrated his own commitment to God's Kingdom with parables about a man planning to build a tower and a king contemplating war. The former would need to cost the project before he began, to avoid the embarrassment of having to abandon it unfinished; the latter would need to assess the relative strengths of his own and his opponent's armies to avoid vain defeat. Jesus' point was that he, the Son of God, had understood the options and had 'forsaken all' to pursue his mission. And he expected the same level of practical, day-by-day commitment from those who would follow him. 'So therefore, any one of you who does not renounce all that he has cannot be my disciple.'

After Paul had described Jesus' downward aspirations, he reminded the Christians at Philippi how he had followed a similar path. Few people had more right than Paul to boast in his social status and intellect. He was born into a prominent Jewish family as a Roman citizen; he trained as a Jewish scholar and could have excelled in either the civil and religious establishment had he not become a disciple of Jesus of Nazareth. 'I count everything as loss because of the surpassing worth of knowing Christ Jesus my Lord', he wrote. 'For his sake I have suffered the loss of all things and count them as rubbish...' The Greek word Paul used actually means something worse than 'rubbish' and so does not appear in many English-language translations. It really means excrement.

If that were not enough, Paul endured hardship in his ministry. He described his life in 1 Corinthians 4:11-13, 2 Corinthians 6:3-10 & 11:21-28. He wrote about being hungry and thirsty, inappropriately dressed, assaulted and homeless. He tells of his endurance through 'afflictions, hardships, calamities, beatings, imprisonments, riots, labours, sleepless nights, hunger...through honour and dishonour, through slander and praise...' He was specific about some details. 'Five times I received at the hands of the Jews the forty lashes less one. Three times I was beaten with rods. Once I was stoned. Three times I was shipwrecked; a night and a day I was adrift at sea; on frequent journeys, in danger from rivers, danger from robbers, danger from my own people, danger from Gentiles, danger in the city, danger in the wilderness, danger at sea, danger from false brothers; in toil and hardship, through many a sleepless night, in hunger and thirst, often without food, in cold and exposure...'

After Jesus had described his own commitment, he repeated an illustration from the Sermon on the Mount, likening his followers to salt. 'Salt is good, but if salt has lost its taste, how shall its saltiness be restored? It is of no use either for the soil or for the manure pile. It is thrown away.' Salt works as a preservative and flavouring only by retaining its distinctiveness. Central to adopting Kingdom principles is a right attitude to money and so Christians who are pretty much indistinguishable from the rest of society lack the distinctiveness to make a difference, either to help introduce individual people to know Jesus or to maintain the moral integrity of society.

While describing his, Paul also explained something of his method: 'By purity, knowledge, patience, kindness, the Holy Spirit, genuine love; by truthful speech, and the power of God; with the weapons of righteousness for the right hand and for the left...' (2 Corinthians 6:6-7). These are not the ways of contemporary society! Later in the letter, Paul explained that, 'For though we walk in the flesh, we are not waging war according to the flesh. For the weapons of our warfare are not of the flesh but have divine power to destroy strongholds. We destroy arguments and every lofty opinion raised against the knowledge of God...' (2 Corinthians 10:3-5). That is the impact of living as Jesus described, the potential for those who consider themselves citizens of the Kingdom of God and live accordingly.

By the time Jesus had finished describing his mission, a crowd had gathered. In particular, he had attracted the attention of the 'tax collectors and sinners', the very people the Pharisees looked down on. This annoyed the Pharisees. I think we can infer from their criticism that he ate with sinners that Jesus had previously left the Pharisee's banquet without eating anything, preferring more sincere hospitality elsewhere.

Speaking to the crowd, Jesus used three parables to explain his mission: a shepherd going a great distance to find a lost sheep, a woman diligently searching her home for a lost coin and a dysfunctional family. Crucially, in the third of these parables Jesus was reaching out not just to the acknowledged 'sinners' in society but to the self-righteous Pharisees also. This is now known as the Parable of the Prodigal Son that is recorded in Luke 15:11-32 but it is as much about the father's love and the elder brother's self-righteousness.

There was a man who had two sons. And the younger of them said to his father, 'Father, give me the share of property that is coming to me.' And he divided his property between them. Not many days later, the younger son gathered all he had and took a journey into a far country, and there he squandered his property in reckless living. And when he had spent everything, a severe famine arose in that country, and he began to be in need. So he went and hired himself out to one of the citizens of that country, who sent him into his fields to feed pigs. And he was longing to be fed with the pods that the pigs ate, and no one gave him anything.

But when he came to himself, he said, 'How many of my father's hired servants have more than enough bread, but I perish here with hunger! I will arise and go to my father, and I will say to him, "Father, I have sinned against heaven and before you. I am no longer worthy to be called your son. Treat me as one of your hired servants."' And he arose and came to his father. But while he was still a long way off, his father saw him and felt compassion, and ran and embraced him and kissed him. And the son said to him, 'Father, I have sinned against heaven and before you. I am no longer worthy to be called your son.' But the father said to his servants, 'Bring quickly the best robe, and put it on him, and put a ring on his hand, and shoes on his feet. And bring the fattened calf and kill it, and let us eat and celebrate. For this my son was dead, and is alive again; he was lost, and is found.' And they began to celebrate.

The family in this story were wealthy landowners. An inheritance would not be divided equally between the sons but the elder would get twice as much as the younger. Although it was insulting for the younger son to ask for his inheritance *before* his father had died, the father would have paid over a third of the value of the estate. The younger son then set off to make his fortune, acting on the same ambition that gripped Lucifer.

The younger son in the parable wanted to be *like* his father. He wanted independence and autonomy, to make his own way and to succeed on his own terms. He did not want to enjoy the good things at home under his father's care but to assert his independence and make his own success. People tend to reject God not because they think that he is bad but because he is in charge.

To be prodigal is to be generous. When the younger son settled away from his father's home and influence, he began to spend his money entertaining other people. In this, he may have been trying to be like his father who would have been a leading figure in society. But, unlike his father, he 'squandered his property in reckless living'. This does not necessarily imply behaviour any worse than people were used to seeing but it was reckless! The people he tried to impress were probably not worth impressing but, like himself, trying to boast their achievements. Many businesspeople today are like that. They spend a lot of money networking to impress their peers and the people they think can profit them in some way. Eventually, inevitably, the prodigal's money ran out, as many people today suddenly discover when their credit card is rejected.

Away from home, the prodigal had nobody to turn to. He soon found himself feeding pigs, a job that no respectable Jew would even consider doing. He was so very hungry that he wanted to eat the pigs own food! Eventually, 'he came to himself'. He realised that he would be better off back at home working as a servant for his father. Which is, of course, exactly where he had started: although he had not been a servant, he had *felt* like one.

As the younger son neared home, he saw his father running out to meet him and, seeming to ignore his son's explanation, drew his son back into the house, not as a servant but as a *son*. The young man did not even get the chance to make his offer of service. A splendid robe covered his rags, a ring restored his status and preparations began immediately for a party. That is how pleased the father was to see his son!

The young son should never have left home but been content to live as a son on his father's estate. Working with the pigs, he came to realise that he could be content working back home as a servant but, until that moment of enlightenment, he had craved autonomy. What is particularly interesting is that this *same* attitude was displayed by the elder brother. He had stayed at home and continued working on the estate but he felt more like a servant than a son. This is how Jesus concluded the parable.

> *Now his older son was in the field, and as he came and drew near to the house, he heard music and dancing. And he called one of the servants and asked what these things meant. And he said to him, 'Your brother has come, and your father has killed the fattened calf, because he has received him back safe and sound.' But he was angry and refused to go in. his father came out and entreated him, but he answered his father, 'Look, these many years I have served you, and I never disobeyed your command, yet you never gave me a young goat, that I might celebrate with my friends. But when this son of yours came, who has devoured your property with prostitutes, you killed the fattened calf for him!' And he said to him, 'Son, you are always with me, and all that is mine is yours.*

When the elder son found his father celebrating his brother's return, he was indignant. He complained that in all the years he had served his father he had never disobeyed him and yet had not been given so much as a young calf for a party for his friends. But the words that must have hurt the father the most were, 'These many years I have *served* you'.

The father reminded his son that he was, in fact, a *son*. Everything on the estate was at his disposal to enjoy. The reality was that as the younger son had already received his inheritance, the rest of the estate, everything the elder son was working on, would pass to him. The tragedy implicit in their conversation is that the elder son never had thought about how dearly he was loved; the tragedy in the real world is that many people fail to see how much God loves them or appreciate the wonder of everything that is available to them.

Without waiting for comment, but on the basis that the meaning of the parable was clear to his audience, Jesus immediately presses on with another parable, one that is today probably the most misunderstood of all his parables. We misunderstand it because our attitudes to money and our beliefs about how business should be conducted are very different today.

> *There was a rich man who had a manager, and charges were brought to him that this man was wasting his possessions. And he called him and said to him, 'What is this that I hear about you? Turn in the account of your management, for you can no longer be manager.' And the manager said to himself, 'What shall I do, since my master is taking the management away from me? I am not strong enough to dig, and I am ashamed to beg. I have decided what to do, so that when I am removed from management, people*

may receive me into their houses.' So, summoning his master's debtors one by one, he said to the first, 'How much do you owe my master?' he said, 'A hundred measures of oil.' he said to him, 'Take your bill, and sit down quickly and write fifty.' Then he said to another, 'And how much do you owe?' he said, 'A hundred measures of wheat.' he said to him, 'Take your bill, and write eighty.' The master commended the dishonest manager for his shrewdness. For the sons of this world are more shrewd in dealing with their own generation than the sons of light. And I tell you, make friends for yourselves by means of unrighteous wealth, so that when it fails they may receive you into the eternal dwellings.

The crucial thing to remember about the dishonest manager is that he was dishonest even when doing the right thing: he was dishonest because he only ever thought of himself!

At the start of the story, he was accused of *wasting* his master's goods. He was not accused of theft, fraud or any 'serious' dishonesty because, had he been, his master would *not* have told him to make up the accounts but immediately put him in prison until everything was repaid! As the accusation means 'squandering', I expect the manager was at fault for commonplace slacking and pilfering, the sort of behaviour that employees in every generation expect to get away with. But while it was not serious dishonesty, it was a taste of the profound dishonesty that would follow when the manager found himself under pressure.

We should be clear that the manager was *not* dishonest for reducing the debts owed to his master. This was within his delegated authority. In fact, it was the right thing to do! In the culture of that place and time, a manager had dual responsibility towards his master and the people with whom his master did business. This responsibility went beyond the commercial prudence exercised today by managers who reduce or waive debts to retain otherwise good customers and clients who are experiencing temporary difficulties. Those are financial decisions made to maintain profitability, not acts of human compassion.

The debtors in Jesus' parable were probably the master's tenants who owed rent, although they may have been customers who owed payment for goods. The manager was responsible for the master's business and, consequently, he was responsible for the welfare of not just the tenants and others who did business with his master but also for the welfare of their families. Making the reductions was therefore both morally right and the responsible social action: the rich creditor who did not need the money reduced the amounts owed by poor people who did.

The manager was dishonest because he reduced the debts *for his own selfish ends*. He did the right thing but he did it in order to fulfil his own need and secure his own future. He did not care about his master's reputation or the welfare of the debtors but for himself only.

The master commended the manager's shrewdness. It is interesting, however, that the Greek word translated shrewdly could also be translated as wisely. It is the adverb of a word that appears 14 times in the New Testament and is almost always translated as 'wise', although it can mean both good and bad wisdom, implying both craftiness as well as discernment. Some translators therefore put 'shrewdly' because they do not want Jesus to appear to be commending the manager's dishonesty as wisdom. But that is to miss the point.

Jesus did **not** commend the manager in any way; he said only that the manager's master commended it. The reason the master commended it, as Jesus went on to explain, was that the 'children of this world' — that is, people who live by the standards of contemporary society — are more shrewd than the 'children of light' — that is, God's people. Jesus acknowledged that the master who lived by society's standards recognised in his manager the sort of wisdom, the sort of craftiness, that society applauded! The master saw something new in his manager and realised that he could be very profitable if his 'shrewdness' were channelled to the master's own advantage.

Did Jesus intend his followers to imitate the manager's shrewdness? In his parables, Jesus always pointed out when a character behaved badly and, in this one, he called the manager dishonest for good reason. So the answer must be, **No!** Jesus did *not* intend his followers to be shrewd like the dishonest manager. He did not want them to act selfishly but self*less*ly. Jesus wants us to do the right thing because it is the right thing to do and not because it is convenient or profitable. This is an important point and this entire book turns on it.

Jesus did not want his followers to be wise like everyone else; he did not want them to be shrewd in the ways of society. He wanted them to be shrewd in the ways of the Kingdom of God. He wanted them to be 'Kingdom shrewd'. I am sure that Jesus' original audience understood him correctly. Do we? In a sermon preached 100 years ago on godly living in godless times, G Campbell Morgan challenged the businesspeople in his congregation not to be content with a superficial Christian witness in their business activities.

I am not suggesting that a man of business is to ask every man who comes into his office if he is a Christian. That is not my suggestion. I am not suggesting that a man on his professional duties shall offer tracts to men. That is not my suggestion. If I were a businessman and you talked to me about my soul when I am doing business with you, I should show you the door immediately. A tract enclosed with an invoice is an insult to religion. When a godly man does business with a godless man, he must see to it that his business is done in a godly fashion.

The godly fashion is not merely the fashion of the man who is strictly just; it is also the fashion of the man who is walking in love. The godly fashion of doing business is not merely the fashion of the man who will refuse to misrepresent his goods. The godly fashion is the fashion of the man who will not allow the other man to sell him something for less than its value in order that he may get the advantage. Oh! you say, I had a great bargain this week. Did you? What was it? I bought a picture and the man did not know its value, but I did. That is not godliness; it is godlessness. Godliness in business means more than integrity and uprightness of purpose. The actually godly man will see that the other man is not wronged or harmed. Every godless man is an opportunity for our godliness to shine forth.

The very things that make it hard to be a Christian are the things which enable us to shine, are opportunities to display the meaning of Christianity and the value of our relationship to God.

We come now to the moment during that difficult day when Jesus spoke the quotation at the start of this chapter. He said that someone who is faithful in what is least is faithful also in much and that a person who is unjust in what is least is unjust in much also. When Jesus told the Pharisees, 'Make friends for yourselves by means of unrighteous wealth [literally, unrighteous mammon], so that when it fails they may receive you into the eternal dwellings', he was not telling them to continue making money as before, shrewd in the ways of the society, so they could use it to help others. That sort of thinking is not only foolish but also dangerous, yet generations of Christians have fallen into that trap.

One of the great myths of capitalism is that when business is free to generate profit, everyone benefits. As money increases, it lifts everyone together on the rising tide of prosperity. This is not often the case, as we can see from the growing gap between rich and poor. But, in any event, it is madness for Christians to buy into the mythology! The primary purpose of trade is to serve communities and to do it in a way to earn enough to live on. That is very different to trading for *maximum* profit. The former is one way of loving our neighbours as ourselves; the latter is to love ourselves very much more than our neighbours. Indeed, it is to *exploit* our neighbours!

Focusing on profit can draw Christians into the same sort of behaviour that is common in modern business. The pursuit of money will foster a love of money that will inevitably lead to serving money. Avarice makes us vulnerable to many other sins and our best ideals are soon abandoned. When I questioned one Christian leader about trying to attract funding with exaggerated claims about what he and his charity were doing, he replied that if his behaviour was not illegal it could not be sinful!

We can perhaps discern the intensity of our blindness to the influence of money today with two examples from the men and women known today as the Desert Fathers. When the Roman Empire 'nationalised' Christianity, making it the official State religion, the Desert Fathers responded by retreating into the hard isolation of the desert to live as monks and hermits. While I cannot endorse all they did and taught, their discipleship was not compromised by financial concerns.

One of them was Evagrios the Solitary. 'When buying or selling', he wrote, 'you can hardly avoid sin. So, in either case, be sure you lose a little in the transaction. Do not haggle about the price for love of gain, and so indulge in actions harmful to the soul — quarrelling, lying, shifting your ground and so on — thus bringing our way of life into disrepute.'

These Christians supported themselves by making things they could sell at market, in order to get the money they needed to buy food and other supplies. One of them sold what he made to the people who needed them the most for whatever price they could afford and then bought what he needed from the people who most needed his custom, for whatever price they asked.

It is too easy to dismiss this carefulness with money as irrelevant to life today. Although the markets where the Desert Fathers traded were less sophisticated than markets today, the traders were no less unscrupulous. Traders have always deceived their customers and disadvantaged their competitors using false weights and measures! The degree to which we, today, can live as Jesus described will depend on the extent to which we, like the Desert Fathers, trust God to underwrite our obedience. I am sure that if more Christians used money with the same caution, the Gospel would be held in greater respect around the world.

As we have already seen in earlier chapters, many of the Pharisees accumulated their wealth dishonestly but what made their money profoundly wicked was their love for it. They claimed to love God but they actually loved money. It was their attitude to their money that had to change, *even if they had become rich honestly and ethically.* Even if, like the dishonest manager, they had done the right thing! Their model should have been a reformed tax collector! They should have used what they had accumulated as Zacchaeus had done and then, like Zacchaeus, lived righteously. Instead, they derided and ridiculed Jesus.

Jesus responded, 'You are those who justify yourselves before men, but God knows your hearts. For what is highly esteemed among men is an abomination in the sight of God.' He went on to explain that people need to 'press into' the Kingdom of God but likened the Pharisees to adulterers! 'Whoever divorces his wife and marries another commits adultery; and whoever marries her who is divorced from her husband commits adultery.' This was not a digression, inserting into the conversation some guidance on divorce and remarriage, but illustrating how the Pharisees had effectively divorced God and married money. *They were guilty of spiritual adultery!*

The Hebrew word for adultery and fornication appears about one hundred times in the Old Testament but in over half of the passages it refers to spiritual, not sexual, sin. Often, this spiritual adultery had a financial motive. The unfaithfulness mentioned towards the end of Psalm 73 is the Hebrew word meaning prostitution but it has nothing to do with sex. The entire Psalm is about people who prosper in spite of their wickedness. James calls his readers 'adulterers and adulteresses' but his letter addresses the disloyalty, divisions and discord caused by *financial* sin.

When Jesus said the Pharisees were like men who divorce their wives to marry their lovers, he was using the same metaphor that Jeremiah used to expresses God's astonishment at Israel's greed (Jeremiah 2-3). Thinking about disloyalty to God as adultery is the corollary of the image of believers as being married to God. This relationship was implied in the Old Testament, although it was more like a formal marriage based on a prenuptial agreement than a love match. The Israelites were repeatedly unfaithful and the prophet Hosea famously married a prostitute to illustrate their persistent adultery (Hosea 1:2). The New Testament describes the Church as the Christ's Bride and the final book in the Bible, Revelation, describes the marriage feast!

Luke continues his account of the Sabbath with Jesus telling the story of Lazarus and the rich man that we touched on in the last chapter. There, we noted that the rich man's offence was not ignoring Lazarus, his neighbour, but of not loving him as himself. Jesus goes further, however, and concludes the story by describing the eternal destiny of both men.

When Lazarus and the rich man died, the former went to be with Abraham in Paradise but the latter found himself in a place of torment. Even in such agony, the rich man still acted like a rich man! He remained narrow-minded and still expected someone to serve him: amazingly, he did not ask to escape his torment, only that Lazarus take him a sip of water!

The poor man [Lazarus] died and was carried by the angels to Abraham's side. The rich man also died and was buried, and in Hades, being in torment, he lifted up his eyes and saw Abraham far off and Lazarus at his side. And he called out, 'Father Abraham, have mercy on me, and send Lazarus to dip the end of his finger in water and cool my tongue, for I am in anguish in this flame.' But Abraham said, 'Child, remember that you in your lifetime received your good things, and Lazarus in like manner bad things; but now he is comforted here, and you are in anguish. And besides all this, between us and you a great chasm has been fixed, in order that those who would pass from here to you may not be able, and none may cross from there to us.' And he said, 'Then I beg you, father, to send him to my father's house — for I have five brothers — so that he may warn them, lest they also come into this place of torment.' But Abraham said, 'They have Moses and the Prophets; let them hear them.' And he said, 'No, father Abraham, but if someone goes to them from the dead, they will repent.' he said to him, 'If they do not hear Moses and the Prophets, neither will they be convinced if someone should rise from the dead.'

In the story, Abraham represents God. The rich man seemed to accept his fate as inevitable but asked Abraham to send someone back from the dead to warn his brothers about what awaited them. Abraham refused, explaining that it is enough that they have 'Moses and the Prophets', by which he meant the Scriptures. The rich man pressed his point: they would listen to someone who had been raised from the dead. Abraham disagreed: even a person returned from death would fail to persuade them.

We now know that what Abraham said in the story is true in the real world because generations have failed to listen to Jesus of Nazareth, who did return from the dead!

Luke's record of that difficult day ends with Jesus warning his disciples — not the Pharisees, or the crowd, but those closest to him — against temptations to sin. He warned them not to put temptation before others but to rebuke and forgive those who do. They asked him to increase their faith but Jesus explained how even just a little faith will grow. But we must not forget the Parables of the Sower and the young plants choked by the deceitfulness of riches, the cares of this world, the pleasures of life and the desire for things!

While we are free to enjoy the good things that come our way and accept hospitality from rich people, we must guard against being drawn into a way of life that looks on them as defining our worth as human beings. As Paul explained it to the Christians in Galatia, 'For you were called to freedom, brothers. Only do not use your freedom as an opportunity for the flesh, *but through love serve one another.* For the whole Law is fulfilled in one word: *"you shall love your neighbour as yourself".'* (Galatians 5:13-14). This involves getting and using money with the same sort of caution that the Desert Fathers demonstrated.

Finally, Jesus reminded his disciples that doing their duty as servants qualified them for no special privilege: 'So you also, when you have done all that you were commanded, say, "We are unworthy servants; we have only done what was our duty".' This reminds me of Paul writing to the church at Corinth, explaining why he preached and taught without seeking the financial remuneration he was entitled to.

I am sure the corrupt Pharisees who Jesus challenged thought they were being wise, or shrewd, mixing religious devotion with their love of money. But they were blind to their own sin. They were unfaithful adulterers, no better than men who audaciously divorced their wives to marry their mistresses. It should be a warning to all of us, even as it raises a host of difficult questions about our lives, with no easy answers to hide behind.

Should we earn money in ways that do not make a positive contribution to society; not just avoiding activities that cause harm or perpetuate injustice but anything that falls short of loving others as we love ourselves? Should we take part in business activity that relies on exploiting people by exaggerating goods or services, like so much marketing, advertising and sales talk do? Should we do anything to benefit from other people's misfortune, like increasing prices in times of tragedy, shortage or need? Should we seek to deceive people by embellishing actual performance or attainable potential in order to get customers, clients or credit? Should we use psychological tactics to create emotional pressure to persuade people to spend or borrow? Should we rely on misdirection and convenient irrelevancies to evade responsibility for errors and poor service? Should we buy things cheaply, knowing that people in poor countries were exploited to produce them?

In the first Christian sermon, preached by Peter at Pentecost, he told the Jews gathered in Jerusalem, 'Save yourselves from this crooked generation' (Acts 2:40). In his letter to the Christians at Philipp, Paul wrote, 'Do all things without grumbling or questioning, that you may be blameless and innocent, *children of God without blemish in the midst of a crooked and twisted generation*, among whom you shine as lights in the world... (Philippians 2:14-15). The meaning of the word crooked is not limited to criminality but to a way of life that is warped and perverse. Christians can leave behind those ways to live transparently reasonable, blameless and innocent lives; faithful with what Jesus called 'the least' and capable of being trusted with 'much'; living as lights in the world, shining brightly.

6: Lay up for yourselves treasures in heaven

Do not lay up for yourselves treasures on earth, where moth and rust destroy and where thieves break in and steal; but lay up for yourselves treasures in heaven, where neither moth nor rust destroys and where thieves do not break in and steal.
Matthew 6:19-20

IN HIS SERMON on the Mount, Jesus told his followers to lay up 'treasure in heaven', not on earth; later, he told a rich young ruler to give all his wealth to the poor, so that he might have this treasure. Also in the Sermon, and in some of his parables, Jesus referred to this treasure as reward.

What is treasure in heaven? We have already glimpsed it in Jesus' parables. It begins with a welcome more magnificent than any king or queen could give us. God himself will say, 'Well done, good and faithful servant'! Will God say that to everyone? I doubt it. Then, because Jesus illustrated our reward, our treasure, as responsibility over cities, we will be given responsibility in the Kingdom of God that that we exercise in fellowship with Jesus.

On the occasion when Jesus' disciples had said that they had given up everything to follow Jesus, he said, 'Truly, I say to you, in the new world, when the Son of Man will sit on his glorious throne, you who have followed me will also sit on twelve thrones, judging the twelve tribes of Israel' (Matthew 19:28). In one of the letters from Jesus in Revelation, he promises that 'The one who conquers, I will grant him to sit with me on my throne, as I also conquered and sat down with my Father on his throne' (Revelation 3:21).

Writing to the Corinthian church, Paul reminded them, 'Do you not know that the saints will judge the world? ... Do you not know that we are to judge angels? (1 Corinthians 6:2-3). Other New Testament letters referred to heavenly rewards as crowns: see, for example, 1 Corinthians 9:24-25, 2 Timothy 4:8, James 1:12 & 1 Peter 5:4; see also Revelation 2:10 & 3:11. Centuries before, Daniel had a vision: 'As I looked...the Ancient of Days came, and judgment was given for the saints of the Most High, and the time came when the saints possessed the kingdom.' (Daniel 7:21-22).

These are just snippets of information about the future but they are reliable, instructive and should inspire us to accumulate treasure in heaven. We are to live in this world so as to be capable of receiving the responsibility — the reward — later.

This raises a very important question that we should consider carefully. Can money buy treasure in heaven? I have often heard it said of money that we cannot take it with us when we die but we can send it on ahead. I know what people mean by that, and I do not wish to seem unduly critical, but it is an over-simplification that I fear could leave a wrong impression. Using money as Jesus described does not 'purchase' heavenly treasure but our obedience to God's ways transforms us into people who can be trusted with it. The 'transformed' people get the treasure they can cope with.

I think it was a 16th Century Christian who likened our reward to jars of varying sizes being filled up. It would have been pointless for the smaller jars to complain that they did not receive as much as the larger ones because each jar was filled to its maximum capacity. That is how it will be for us!

There is, however, a danger that we could, by our lifestyles, forfeit our reward. Peter explained in his first letter that we have 'an inheritance that is imperishable, undefiled, and unfading', kept for us in heaven, and Paul explained in his letters how Christians can lose their reward by indulging in (among other things) theft and swindling, greed and covetousness.

This chapter may represent a turning point in understanding what Jesus taught about money. Up to now, it may have seemed as if there is nothing good about money, that the dangers of having more than enough far outweigh the hardships of not having enough. I know that some people do think that way but money is a tool and all tools are neutral, neither good nor evil but available for use by both good and evil people for both honourable and disgraceful purposes.

A hammer can be used to build or demolish; money can be used to help and bless people or to persecute and abuse them. In this chapter, we look at the right ways to use money: ways that help and bless. It is centred on Jesus' Sermon on the Mount, which has been called the 'manifesto' of the Kingdom of God, and from which is taken the statement about serving God and money that we explored in the first chapter. As I explained there, I think that Jesus wants us to understand that we need not worry about the financial consequences of living as he described. He wants us to live with integrity, dealing with people in a straightforward way, to do good to our rivals and those who would be our enemies and to abound in good works, even when this is dangerous.

On the two occasions that Jesus sent out his disciples to minister on their own, in pairs, he warned them that they were going as 'sheep in the midst of wolves'. But, he added, 'Be wise as serpents and innocent as doves' (see Matthew 10 & Luke 10). As we have seen in previous chapters, to be innocent is not to be naive and our wisdom is not to be the prevailing wisdom of contemporary society. We need to be 'Kingdom shrewd'.

* * *

In the Sermon on the Mount, recorded in Matthew 5:3-7:27, Jesus described how to live in the Kingdom of God. I want to offer now a brief overview of the entire Sermon but, first, we should look again at the passage on money, so that we can keep in mind the financial implications. As I can only make a few general points in this chapter, I hope that it will be an incentive for you to begin to study Jesus' Sermon in a fresh way.

Do not lay up for yourselves treasures on earth, where moth and rust destroy and where thieves break in and steal, but lay up for yourselves treasures in heaven, where neither moth nor rust destroys and where thieves do not break in and steal. For where your treasure is, there your heart will be also.

The eye is the lamp of the body. So, if your eye is healthy, your whole body will be full of light, but if your eye is bad, your whole body will be full of darkness. If then the light in you is darkness, how great is the darkness!

No one can serve two masters, for either he will hate the one and love the other, or he will be devoted to the one and despise the other. You cannot serve God and money.

Therefore I tell you, do not be anxious about your life, what you will eat or what you will drink, nor about your body, what you will put on. Is not life more than food, and the body more than clothing? Look at the birds of the air: they neither sow nor reap nor gather into barns, and yet your heavenly Father feeds them. Are you not of more value than they? And which of you by being anxious can add a single hour to his span of life? And why are you anxious about clothing? Consider the lilies of the field, how they grow: they neither toil nor spin, yet I tell you, even Solomon in all his glory was not arrayed like one of these. But if God so clothes the grass of the field, which today is alive and tomorrow is thrown into the oven, will he not much more clothe you, O you of little faith? Therefore do not be anxious, saying, 'What shall we eat?' or 'What shall we drink?' or 'What shall we wear?' For the Gentiles seek after all these things, and your heavenly Father knows that you need them all. But seek first the kingdom of God and his righteousness, and all these things will be added to you.

Therefore do not be anxious about tomorrow, for tomorrow will be anxious for itself. Sufficient for the day is its own trouble.

This passage sets out Jesus' paradigm for handling money.
- Do not be anxious about material things like food and clothing or, by extension, anything else that money can buy.
- Make seeking God's Kingdom and righteousness the sole lifestyle priority.
- Trust God for basic needs.

Some translations say 'give no thought' to material needs. That was an old fashioned way of saying not to worry or fret but if taken literally today it goes too far. Jesus was warning against anxiety, not sensible forethought and planning. Jesus wants his disciples to make rational lifestyle choices and spending decisions but to base them on what is right, not what is cost effective.

When Paul wrote about the dangers of loving money, he reiterated the same priorities as Jesus but used stronger language to encourage Timothy to orientate his life away from temptation.

> Now there is great gain in godliness with contentment, for we brought nothing into the world, and we cannot take anything out of the world. But if we have food and clothing, with these we will be content. But those who desire to be rich fall into temptation, into a snare, into many senseless and harmful desires that plunge people into ruin and destruction. For the love of money is a root of all kinds of evils. It is through this craving that some have wandered away from the faith and pierced themselves with many pangs. But as for you, O man of God, flee these things. Pursue righteousness, godliness, faith, love, steadfastness, gentleness. Fight the good fight of the faith. Take hold of the eternal life to which you were called and about which you made the good confession in the presence of many witnesses.

This guidance in 1 Timothy 6:6-12 can be summed up like this.
- Be content with the necessary things in life, like food and clothing, and keep to your faith in God.
- Flee desires, like avarice and covetousness: do not just ignore them but do what you can to put yourself beyond their reach.
- Pursue righteousness, godliness, faith, love, steadfastness and gentleness: do not just seek them but *chase* them and grasp eternal life.

That money should be of secondary importance in life is not a unique Christian position. Many philosophers and religious teachers believe that when we want to do the right thing that the money necessary to do it will become available. There may be some truth in that belief, because of the way God created the world to operate and designed humans to live together in it, but I am a Christian and believe in a LORD God who actively underwrites our commitment to the way of life he wants us to live. The challenge is for us to live as Jesus described with this assurance. If God fails to sustain us, then the problem is with either our understanding of his purpose or our ability to see the bigger picture.

After telling his disciples to accumulate treasure in heaven, Jesus told them that where their treasure was their heart would be also. Paul said much the same thing when he wrote, 'If then you have been raised with Christ, *seek the things that are above*, where Christ is, seated at the right hand of God. *Set your minds on things that are above, not on things that are on earth.* For you have died, and your life is hidden with Christ in God. When Christ who is your life appears, *then you also will appear with him in glory*' (Colossians 3:1-4).

Writing to the church at Philippi, Paul warned, 'For many...walk as enemies of the cross of Christ. Their end is destruction, their god is their belly, and they glory in their shame, *with minds set on earthly things*' (Philippians 3:18-20). He described Christians largely indifferent to treasure in heaven! He concluded the passage, 'But our citizenship is in heaven...' By contrast he wrote of Timothy, 'For I have no one like him, *who will be genuinely concerned for your welfare*. For they all seek their own interests, not those of Jesus Christ. But you know Timothy's proven worth...' (Philippians 2:20-22)

Jesus explained how serving money affects our lives, distorting our vision. If our eyes are healthy, able to see the spiritual as well as the material, our bodies can be full of light; but if our eyes are blinded by the materialism, capitalism and consumerism around us, our bodies will be full of darkness. If 'light' inside us is mammon's glow, how great is our darkness!

Human nature, natural avarice, the social pressure to succeed and workplace challenges pull us more towards vices than virtues. It is, therefore, no wonder if we cannot see where we are, know what is right or the right thing to do! Just as brightly lit shop displays tempt us to accumulate stuff we neither need nor wanted, so television, movies and magazines illuminate and glamorise celebrity vices like conceit, boasting, jealousy, deceit, bravado, ostentation, sexuality, lust, insensitivity, callousness, cruelty and hubris. Cast in a favourable light, mammon's light, selfishness and greed take on the appearance of prudence; vanity and pride can look like commendable smartness.

How important is it for you to lay up sufficient treasure on earth, so that you feel secure about your future? How easily is your desire for ease, elegance and entertainment exploited by advertising and sales talk? How vulnerable are you to concerns about your credibility, reputation and status? Does status anxiety rob you of contentment? To what extent does peer pressure motivate your spending? I do not think that any of us can be complacent that we are immune to the influences that are everywhere around us!

A few years ago, after I taught about the financial implications of the Sermon on the Mount to an audience of about 100 people, I was congratulated on my eisegesis.

But I was not quite sure whether it was a sincere compliment! Eisegesis is reading our own ideas into a Bible passage. It is the opposite of exegesis, which is to draw out the ideas from a passage. While exegesis is greatly admired among preachers and teachers, eisegesis is usually derided. I therefore ask you to keep an open mind as to whether I properly understand what Jesus said and am not reading my own ideas into it.

Jesus went up the 'mount' to teach his immediate disciples. This was a larger group than the twelve apostles but, in addition, a great crowd followed and we can assume that many if not all of them overheard what he said. It is unclear to me whether Jesus meant the Sermon just for his immediate disciples or the crowd around them but Jesus often used the phrase, 'He who has ears to hear, let him hear', indicating that his teaching was for everyone who heard it gladly and took it to heart.

The Sermon develops the twin foundational principles of loving God with our entire heart, soul, strength and mind and loving our neighbours as ourselves. Moreover, it sows the seeds for everything else he taught and for all that his early followers taught that is in the New Testament: consider, for example, Galatians 5-6, Ephesians 4-6, Colossians, Titus, James and 1 Peter.

Jesus began with a stunning reversal about who in society is blessed. It was as radical to his original audience as it should be to us. On that hillside in Galilee, the people would have been familiar with the blessings God promised in Deuteronomy 28 if they were faithful to him.

Blessed shall you be in the city, and blessed shall you be in the field. Blessed shall be the fruit of your womb and the fruit of your ground and the fruit of your cattle, the increase of your herds and the young of your flock. Blessed shall be your basket and your kneading bowl. Blessed shall you be when you come in, and blessed shall you be when you go out...The Lord will command the blessing on you in your barns and in all that you undertake...'

But Jesus described blessings that appeared to be reserved for a different group of people.

Blessed are the poor in spirit... Blessed are those who mourn... Blessed are the meek... Blessed are those who hunger and thirst for righteousness... Blessed are the merciful... Blessed are the pure in heart... Blessed are the peacemakers... Blessed are those who are persecuted for righteousness' sake... Blessed are you when others revile you and persecute you and utter all kinds of evil against you falsely on my account...

What Jesus said was not incompatible with the blessings of Deuteronomy 28 but I expect that it *seemed* very different to many in his audience. To be fully human, however, requires our practical living and enjoyment of life to be infused with spiritual insight; knowing that we do our best and use all the technical skill we have, we remain dependent on God alone for the blessings. When we hunger and thirst for righteousness and to make peace, any material abundance we have is the opportunity God gives us to fulfil those desires. As we saw previously, many of the Pharisees squandered their many opportunities!

I imagine that some in the audience began to murmur their disappointment. Jesus assured them that living this way would make them the salt of the earth and the light of the world. Salt prevents corruption and adds flavour; light exposes deceit and danger and illuminates a right, safe way forward. That is the role of Christians in every age and the reason they are often out of step with the rest of society.

Before interpreting key sections of the Law, Jesus warned his disciples — and the crowd around them who were listening — that their righteousness had to exceed the righteousness of the Pharisees. The Pharisees were in many ways the most religious people in Israel but in sticking 'religiously' to the rules most of them failed utterly to please God. As Jesus said on another occasion, 'Woe to you, scribes and Pharisees, hypocrites! For you tithe mint and dill and cumin, and have neglected the weightier matters of the Law: justice and mercy and faithfulness. These you ought to have done, without neglecting the others.' They made sure they gave to God one tenth of every herb they grew but they abused people terribly. They were lovers of money who, under cover of their religion, would 'devour' widows' houses.

'Do not think that I have come to abolish the Law or the Prophets', Jesus said, 'I have not come to abolish them but to fulfil them.' It is easy, very easy, for those of us who are not Jews to underestimate these words! The Law was the Torah, the teaching of life, the sum and summary of all that God expected of his people that had stood unchallenged for centuries.

Generations of Jewish scholars had interpreted and applied the Law, often to the point where they reversed the original intention. That is how they came to criticise Jesus for healing people on holy days! But no scholar or teacher would ever dare try to set it aside. For Jesus of Nazareth even to suggest that people might think this was his intention would have been perceived as the most arrogant presumption!

But then Jesus was even more outrageous! He said that he had come to *fulfil* the Law and the Prophets, to do *everything* that God expects of people! That would have sounded like blasphemy! I suspect that the only thing that kept people listening was the unmistakable authority with which Jesus spoke. At the end of the Sermon, Matthew records that, 'the people were astonished at his teaching, for he taught them as one having authority, and not as the scribes'. I think his unique authority kept Jesus from being stoned that day!

Jesus fulfilled the Law and the Prophets by keeping every detail of it but it is important to remember that Jesus did not keep it as the scribes and Pharisees understood it. He fulfilled it all as God intended it. He did not fulfil it theoretically or legalistically but inherently and profoundly: he lived it God's way as only God the Son, the Messiah, could live it.

In the Sermon, Jesus taught God's ways, correcting many of the interpretations of the Law developed by Jewish scholars. On another occasion, Jesus explained that, 'The words that I say to you I do not speak on my own authority, but the Father who dwells in me does his works' (John 14:10). Jesus emphasised the spirit, not the letter, describing lifestyle not legalisation. This is why he went on to say, 'Unless your righteousness *exceeds* that of the scribes and Pharisees, you will never enter the kingdom of heaven'. Would-be disciples of Jesus of Nazareth needed a better righteousness than the best of the Pharisees, not to be more scrupulous in their adherence to the dos and don'ts but to absorb God's ways into their thinking and behaviour.

Jesus began his restatement of God's ways with the relationships between his own disciples. He said, 'You have heard that it was said to those of old, "You shall not murder; and whoever murders will be liable to judgment" But I say to you that everyone who is angry with his brother will be liable to judgment; whoever insults his brother will be liable to the council; and whoever says, 'You fool!' will be liable to the hell of fire.'

Jesus' use of the word 'brother' should not be overlooked or underestimated. The statement is not directed to Christians who causes offence but to the offended who might be tempted to respond in anger. On another occasion, recounted in Matthew 18:15-35, Jesus went a step further to direct the offended ones to seek reconciliation.

It is easy to see why this is foundational to everything that followed in the Sermon. It is not only a very clear example of how a command about behaviour must be internalised and taken to heart but, as we saw in Chapter 4, it is disciples' love for one another that is to distinguish us from the rest of society.

There will be, inevitably, occasions when Christians upset each other but the person who is offended is not to resort to anger and name-calling. The importance of this is why Paul had to write so strongly to the Corinthian church, telling the Christians there to refrain from legal action and sort out their own problems. Unfortunately, today the rivalry between many churches and between Christians within churches ranges from terrible wars of words to cold indifference, all of which taints their public witness, undermines their ability to make disciples and hinders revival.

I accept that Christians will have differences about theology and practice, and that sometimes those differences can run deep, but that can be no excuse for a lack of mutual love and practical help. As James reminded his readers, 'Let every person be quick to hear, slow to speak, slow to anger; for the anger of man does not produce the righteousness of God' (James 1:20). Paul went further when he wrote, 'Live in harmony with one another… Repay no one evil for evil, but give thought to do what is honourable in the sight of all. If possible, so far as it depends on you, live peaceably with all' (Romans 12:16-18).

This sort of advice can be hard to follow, especially if it involves financial loss or requires us to give money to fellow Christians we profoundly disagree with. But it is the starting point only, the very least we should do. For Christians to be salt and light, we need to distinguish ourselves as true disciples of Jesus of Nazareth and the *sole* criteria that Jesus gave for this is our love for one another: please take a moment to read again John 13:34-35.

After addressing his disciples' relationship with each other, Jesus describes how they are to relate to the rest of society. This is how Christians are to live shrewdly by the ways of the Kingdom of God. I find this division helpful when reflecting on the financial implications: sex, integrity, reasonableness, adversaries and good works.

Sex. (Matthew 5:27-32) Although Jesus is talking primarily about faithfulness in marriage, it has implications for everyone living in a society where lust is an effective means of selling goods and services. The provocations are more insidious than just the images of glamorous, charismatic men and women used in advertising.

The natural wish to be accepted, liked and fulfilled is exploited by unnatural preoccupation with body shape and sexual attraction, so that people think to bolster their self-confidence by spending. Illusions of happy families manipulate people into buying household items, cars, holidays and anything else that will mark them out as good spouses and parents.

In many sections of society today, the enjoyment of pornography is commonplace and sexual intercourse is something to be enjoyed with no more self-restrain than alcohol. Christians tend to think they do well guarding against these attitudes but it usually hinders only to the more visible acts: discrete behaviour, like addiction to pornography and adulterous flings on business trips, tend to be ignored.

Integrity. (Matthew 5:33-37) When Jesus said, 'Let what you say be simply 'Yes' or 'No'; anything more than this comes from evil', he went beyond any sense of superficial truthfulness. When we equate truth with honesty, as so many people do today, we can convince ourselves that it is not dishonest to mislead with partial truth. People therefore blag, distract, trick, mislead, misdirect, distort, evade, fabricate, exaggerate and embellish but they do not lie; they mix euphemism, abstraction, expectation, understatement, metaphor and slang to create an illusion that cannot be sustained under scrutiny.

Integrity needs to be profound to be viable. It includes personal wholeness, general soundness and being true to ourselves and our values. And, concurrently, seeking to ensure that our values are real and true and not just convenient to us for the time being. Of course, we should not reveal things to people who have no right to know them but we should, nonetheless, deal with them in a reliable and straightforward way.

Reasonableness. (Matthew 5:38-42) Just as Jesus had told his disciples not to respond to each other in anger, so he now tells them to show the same restraint to anyone else who insults or abuses them. We saw in chapter 4 that Jesus is not here talking about condoning criminality or suggesting that we passively accept all 'legal' injustices, only that we act with constructive, righteous creatively.

Adversaries. (Matthew 5:43-48) Jesus' comments on abuse lead into the obligation to love our enemies. As we have considered before, this is not to expose us to preventable fraud or other harm. We need to be real about the people who hate us but, like the Samaritan who came across the injured Jew, we must act when a need is clear. This includes inconsiderate neighbours, devious work colleagues, deceitful business rivals and unreasonable government officials.

Good works. (Matthew 6:1-4) The important point that Jesus made was that our good deeds should be done quietly, tactfully, unobtrusively — not for public display! When done for that end, the public acclaim may be all the reward we get and the opportunity to accumulate treasure in heaven will have been lost.

Jesus next talks about prayer and our dependence on God alone. Prayers are not to be public displays of spirituality and when we fast we are to keep the matter between God and ourselves. Conspicuous by its absence from the model prayer Jesus taught, what we now call 'The Lord's Prayer', is concern about the many details of daily life. Instead, it focuses on God, his divine majesty and sovereignty in providing our daily needs, and on the obligation on us to forgive as he forgives and to let him guide us. When we can pray this with uncompromised faith in God, a great deal of care and concern about material things is lifted from our shoulders!

Jesus then gets to the heart of the issue of trust and our attitude to money. Do we rely on God or money to meet our daily needs and to fulfil our temporal ambitions? Do we serve God in the ways we live, seeking his eternal Kingdom and doing his righteousness? Or, do we in fact serve money, so that earning it becomes an inescapable lifestyle priority and doing the righteousness Jesus described only if we think we can sustain the financial cost?

The reality is that the only way anyone can live as Jesus described is by proactively relying on God to underwrite our obedience to his ways. 'Ask, and it will be given to you; seek, and you will find; knock, and it will be opened to you', Jesus said. 'For everyone who asks receives, and the one who seeks finds, and to the one who knocks it will be opened.'

Notwithstanding what sounds like an absolute statement from Jesus' own lips, we must acknowledge that we have all prayed for something and not received it. And we have concocted all sorts of reasons to explain why God did not give us what we asked for, whether it was a childhood request for a Christmas present or physical healing for a loved one. The reason for unanswered prayer was explained by James in his letter to feuding Christians: 'You ask and do not receive, because you ask wrongly, to spend it on your passions'. The word, 'spend', means to consume and has a wider relevance than spending money. Many prayers therefore go unanswered because they are ultimately selfish.

We must, however, remember God's wonderful goodness to us and that he always gives us things that we do not deserve to have. We do not 'deserve' even to be counted as Christians! All that God gives he therefore gives in love.

It is easy to focus on Jesus' promise recorded in John 16:23 that. 'Whatever you ask of the Father in my name, he will give it to you' but to forget the context in which he gave it. We have to be abiding in him, as a branch in a vine, as he had explained in the previous chapter. If we do, then, among other things, we will love others as Jesus loves us. It follows that whenever we do not get what we pray for, our reaction should be to assume that the lack is of something that would harm us or to ask ourselves what new thing God wants us to learn.

In the case of the churches that James wrote to, the rich were indifferent to the needs of the poor and the poor were impatient with the rich for their indifference. Their sins were different but neither of the two groups distinguished themselves by their love, as we read in James 4:1-4.

> What causes quarrels and what causes fights among you? Is it not this, that your passions are at war within you? You desire and do not have, so you murder. You covet and cannot obtain, so you fight and quarrel. You do not have, because you do not ask. You ask and do not receive, because you ask wrongly, to spend it on your passions. You adulterous people! Do you not know that friendship with the world is enmity with God?

Did James refer to literal murder? I think so, although not a legal liability that could be established in a court of law. I think the 'murder' he had in mind was the result of the indifference of rich Christians when they failed to intervene to help vulnerable people in need and who then died. This was a failure both to love their fellow Christians in a way that would distinguish them as true disciples of Jesus and of the more general responsibility to love their neighbours as themselves. They were, instead, governed by the same attitude towards money, the same desires for wealth and possessions, as other rich people around them. And they behaved just as badly, even to the point of unjustly withholding their employees' wages (James 5:1-6).

Towards the end of his Sermon on the Mount, Jesus included a warning against being judgemental and the need for discernment. This was to guard us from trying to impose our own standards on others. 'Judge not, that you be not judged... Why do you see the speck that is in your brother's eye, but do not notice the log that is in your own eye? ... You hypocrite, first take the log out of your own eye, and then you will see clearly to take the speck out of your brother's eye... Do not give dogs what is holy, and do not throw your pearls before pigs... (Matthew 7:2-6). We need good judgement but must avoid the sort of judgementalism that fuelled Pharisees sense of superiority.

It was judgementalism that caused the social friction in the churches that James wrote to. While it would seem that there was much to judge in the attitude of the rich Christians, the poor were just as wrong in judging out of jealousy and loathing rather than out of compassion for erring brothers and sisters in Christ. In the event, all of them were the sort of hypocrites that Jesus warned against, so James told them to tame their tongues, exercise 'wisdom from above' and, at the end of the letter, described the true merit of bringing back sinners from their wanderings. I recommend reading the entire letter, keeping in mind the financial provocations.

It is judgementalism that has, on the whole, caused Christians throughout history to divide and fight over doctrine and, in doing so, undermine their own witness. I think the example of many of the Reformers in the 15th & 16th Centuries is tragic: asserting great spiritual truths, they could not tolerate each other. World history would have been very different if they and the Roman Catholics they separated from had loved each other as Jesus commanded.

It is sometimes necessary to judge but important that our vision is clear, neither obscured by our own prejudices and other 'logs' nor obsessed by the 'specks' we see in others. The need for sound judgement is important because Jesus sums up his Sermon with one warning against false prophets and another against superficial discipleship.

The context implies that Jesus' warning covered more than only those who claim a prophetic gift but all sorts of bogus preachers and teachers 'who come to you in sheep's clothing but inwardly are ravenous wolves'! As we are all fallible, this should keep us alert! We too could build fine reputations on sand and end up strangers to Jesus. We might profess allegiance and demonstrate correct understanding, such as 'right' theology; we may teach, preach and prophesy but, at the end, hear him tell us, 'I never knew you'!

On the occasion, recorded in Mark 9:38-40, the disciples asked Jesus whether they should stop the man casting out demons in Jesus' name but who was not part of their group. Jesus said, 'Do not stop him, for no one who does a mighty work in my name will be able soon afterward to speak evil of me. For the one who is not against us is for us.' Could this have been someone who believed in Jesus, was 'for' Jesus but never made the time and personal space in which to get to know Jesus?

One of Jesus' parables about how his disciples should behave while awaiting his return describes ten virgins waiting with a bride for her bridegroom to come to take her to his home to finalise the marriage (Matthew 25:1-13). The bridegroom is symbolic of Jesus, the Son of Man, returning to collect his people, the Church, as he described in Mark 13.

The bridegroom came unexpectedly during the night. Many translations say he arrived at midnight but the Hebrew is not that specific and in Mark 13 Jesus says that he could return at any time from dusk to dawn.

We should not read too much into all the virgins being asleep. Although in Mark 13 Jesus tells his disciples to remain alert during the night, even firefighters and fighter pilots on call sleep if they need to: the important thing is that they are prepared and ready to go as soon as they wake up. In the parable, the five wise virgins had been diligent, were prepared and could join the wedding procession immediately the bridegroom arrived.

The foolish virgins had not been diligent. They had run out of oil and, by the time they had found more, it was too late to join the procession. When they knocked on the banquet door, the bridegroom did not recognise them: 'Truly, I say to you, I do not know you'.

These foolish virgins represent the same people mentioned towards the end of the Sermon on the Mount, so would hear Jesus tell them that he did not know them. Although they might have called him, 'Lord', prophesied, exorcised demons and done other 'mighty works', Jesus said, 'I never knew you; depart from me, you workers of lawlessness'.

It seems very harsh for the bridegroom in the parable to deny knowing the foolish virgins but while waiting for him, they had not been focused on their sole task of preparing: they had been 'lawless'. Perhaps they had just liked to party too much!

It seems harsh, too, for Jesus to call people who had done much in his name 'workers of lawlessness' but, like the foolish virgins, I expect that they had not been properly focused. Or perhaps they had been like the dishonest manager, doing the right things but for selfish motives.

The concept of 'useless', 'wicked' and 'lawless' Christians will always be hard for us to accept but it simply refers to those who serve themselves rather than their master. 'Evil' was how James described the Christian businesspeople who ran their businesses without reference to God and boasted about their success; when Paul writes of the judgment seat of Christ, he is warning Christians that their lives may end up being judged as evil! (James 4:13-17 & 2 Corinthians 5:10).

This does not imply that they were consigned to hell. The Bible gives us to understand that there are different rewards in heaven and I therefore have no difficulty imagining a place there where some Christians have little or no reward and consequently experience profound regret at the way they lived. This may be what Jesus on other occasions referred to as a place of wailing and gnashing of teeth: it may be the time when they are before the Judgement Seat of Christ, where their true selves are exposed — an experience that seems to me to be very different from the welcome extended to the faithful and wise servants in the parables.

I want to push the application of the parable of the virgins a little further. What might have happened if the bridegroom had arrived and not only found five of the virgins not ready but also the bride unprepared? My liberty in suggesting this may not be too far-fetched because it seems to me that Paul suggested something similar.

Paul's Corinthian letters dealt with a variety of issues because those Christians had lost their vision of the Kingdom of God and were trying to live like the rest of Corinthian society but without actually sinning. Of course, they did sin because they reasoned that so very many of the things they wanted to do were 'lawful', even thought they were potentially divisive, addictive and self-destructive: see 1 Corinthians 6:12 & 10:23.

In 2 Corinthians 11:1-4, Paul goes to some lengths to explain why he wanted them to change. 'For I feel a divine jealousy for you, since I betrothed you to one husband, to present you as a pure virgin to Christ. But I am afraid that...your thoughts will be led astray from a sincere and pure devotion to Christ...' Having betrothed the Corinthian Christians to 'one husband', Paul feared they were not fit to be Christ's bride! Rather than be ready for their Bridegroom's arrival, they were living like the rest of Greek society, even attending the worship of pagan idols. They were guilty of spiritual adultery, much of it motivated by the opportunity for financial gain!

Many Christians today expect to be able to enjoy all the good things in life, just like the Christians in Corinth. They go to church, worship, pray and take notes of the sermons; at home, they read the Bible, read 'Christian' books, watch worship and sermons on TV or listen to them on CDs. And they pray. But they do little else! They are, in James' words, hearers not doers of the Word. They may be 'converts' and 'believers' but they are not 'disciples'.

By definition, disciples strive to *live* consistently with all that Jesus taught. At the start of the first chapter, I explained how most of the teaching in the Bible is integrated within books of history, philosophy and poetry. On the whole, God teaches us lifestyle through the lives of people who have gone before us, so that most of

Jesus' teaching is contained in biographies and the letters written by his early followers. Paul explained the usefulness of the Bible in this famous statement (2 Timothy 3:16-17).

All Scripture is breathed out by God and profitable for teaching, for reproof, for correction, and for training in righteousness, that the man of God may be competent, equipped for every good work

Some things in the Bible may be dated and seem irrelevant, as people are often quick to point out, but Paul knew that it is all 'profitable'. I am sure that he chose the word carefully: it means helpful and serviceable. The teaching may be ancient but it remains applicable, to inform and equip us to do good in the world that God created and to prepare for the future that awaits us.

In one of his letters, Peter explained that we have 'an inheritance that is imperishable, undefiled, and unfading, kept in heaven for you' (1 Peter 1:3-5). But Paul explains in his letters how Christians can forsake their inheritance by indulging in certain lifestyle choices. We know from 1 Corinthians 6:9-10, Galatians 5:19-21 and Ephesians 5:1-6 that these choices include covetousness, theft, swindling, jealousy and rivalries.

I think the absence of authentic spiritual authority in much of the world today is because of the way so many Christians and churches trust in money like the otherwise devout Israelites who put Asherah poles in their fields. But when our allegiance to God is uncompromised, we will being trading with the investment he has given us, accumulating treasure in heaven and exercising spiritual authority.

We must beware of making the same mistake of Simon, the former magician, who thought that he could in some way purchase Holy Spirit gifts. We must be careful of hoping that by maxing out our giving we will in some way *earn* or *deserve* greater blessing. But that caution should not keep us from thinking deeply think about what sort of treasure appeals to us more. The latest fashions, restaurant meals and being seen in the 'right' places? Or wisdom, knowledge, faith, generosity, service, teaching, healing, miracles, prophecy, spiritual perception and 'tongues' that can only be empowered by the Holy Spirit?

The primary task that Jesus gave his disciples just before he ascended to heaven was to, 'Go...and make disciples of all nations' (Matthew 28:19-20). To make 'disciples'. But if we are distracted and compromising in our lifestyle, we may be more like the useless, wicked and lawless servants than we care to think and incapable of helping others to be disciples.

We can live in this world either serving God, living his way as described in the Bible, or serving money, the thing that most people today rely on to get things and to get things done. We cannot hope to do both!

Postscript

AMONG THE VISUAL aids I use in my talks are two bank notes and two coins. One of the bank notes is from the United States of America and seems to have a value of $1,000,000. It seems to be so valuable that no American President is worthy of having his face on it and so there is a picture of the Statue of Liberty instead. But, really, it is just a piece of paper. It looks like a real bank note but if you look at it closely it is clear that it is bogus. But although it is a novelty note produced to amuse people, and nobody should be fooled by it, occasionally I hear how somebody tried to spend one or pay one into their bank account.

I also have a genuine bank note issued by Zimbabwe's central bank in 2008 with a face value of $50,000,000. The note is now out of date but even when it was in circulation it did not buy you much — probably much less than a £10 note from the UK.

The two coins were minted in Germany in the 1920s. Each one has a face value of $\mathcal{M}$500,000, but their curiosity value today is greater than their 'real' value in Germany 90 years ago.

The fact is, you can trust money only for as long as everyone else trusts it. You could have a suitcase full of billions of euros but if nobody else trusted in them, you could not use them to buy a chocolate bar. Money is real only because we chose to believe it is real and we need enough other people to believe also for it to be of use to us.

By contrast, we can always trust Jesus Christ of Nazareth, who is 'the same yesterday and today and forever' (Hebrews 13:8). Our belief in him is not dependent on anyone else agreeing with us: we can trust him implicitly and with impunity, whether or not anyone else trusts him. I therefore close this book remembering by what authority he taught.

Jesus of Nazareth is Almighty God, God the Son, the Messiah, Jesus Christ who 'has come in the flesh'. He did not come on a simple rescue mission, to save individual people from hell. Although he did do this, he had a much grander, more comprehensive purpose: to reconcile together into one all things in heaven and earth and then to present them to the Father. To this end, he died on a cross.

Three days later, his Father (God the Father) raised him from the dead 'and seated him at his right hand in the heavenly places, far above all rule and authority and power and dominion, and above every name that is named, not only in this age but also in the one to come. And he put all things under his feet and gave him as head over all things to the church, which is his body, the fullness of him who fills all in all' (see Ephesians 1).

It is on this authority of Jesus Christ that we can live by the standards of the eternal Kingdom of God, not the passing consumer society. Although there is more to this than the ways we get and use money, unless these ways do comply with what Christ taught, then it is certain that we cannot get far seeking God's kingdom and his righteousness.

Appendix: G Campbell Morgan on business

In his first book, *Discipleship*, published in 1897, G Campbell Morgan devoted a chapter to work. This extract about business behaviour is no less relevant to disciples of Jesus Christ today who wish to be 'Kingdom shrewd' at work.

THE DISCIPLE IN business on his own account lives and acts within certain very clearly defined principles. He ever remembers that he is a steward of his Master. He possesses nothing, but holds on trust all he has, and is responsible to Christ for the way he gets, the way he uses, and the measure of his getting or holding. No disciple of Jesus can amass a fortune simply for the sake of possession. He may be prosperous in his undertakings, but his prosperity must ever mean increased opportunity for Divine service. No disciple can oppress the hireling in his wages. That wage should be, not merely the measure of keeping his servant's body and soul together, it should include provision for the culture of all that his being demands. A 'living wage' in the common acceptation of that term, is not the measure for a Christian paymaster.

A Christian cannot consent to enrich himself by taking advantage of the downfall or misfortune of another man. That man who strikes a bargain to his own profit which takes advantage of some pressing need on the part of another, is none of Christ's. No Christian can take part in the monopolies of the day, which have as the very basis of their operations the enrichment of the few to the detriment of the many. There is nothing perhaps more devilish in commercial life today than the great monopolies. America is cursed by them, and England is threatened. No disciple of Christ can touch them and abide in the teaching of Jesus. The twofold law of life, enunciated by our Teacher, will purify commerce throughout, and nothing short of that will ever do it. 'Thou shalt love the Lord thy God with all thy heart, and with all thy soul, and with all thy mind...Thou shalt love thy neighbour as thyself' (Matthew 22:37-40).

These are said to be impossible ideals for business life today. We reply that the very essence and genius of discipleship is the realisation of the impossible. It is just because the Church of Jesus Christ has stood in the presence of His teaching and said 'Impossible' that She has become so weak and forceless in all the affairs of this busy age. Let us have a few men and women again who, like the early disciples in Pentecostal days, believe in Jesus and in the eternal wisdom of all His teaching, and who are prepared to suffer the loss of all things rather than disobey, and the potency and possibility of His ideals will begin to dawn on the world again as it did in those days, breaking up dynasties, revolutionising empires, and turning the world upside down.

Nowhere is such work more needed than in the realm of commerce, and nowhere can we make better investment for the Master's Kingdom today than by purifying rigidly that corner of the great realm which we touch.

Let every disciple find his gift from God, cultivate it for God, exercise it abiding in God, and he will not only secure his own highest success, but will contribute his quota to the preparatory work of this dispensation for the coming of the King and the establishment of His Kingdom on earth.